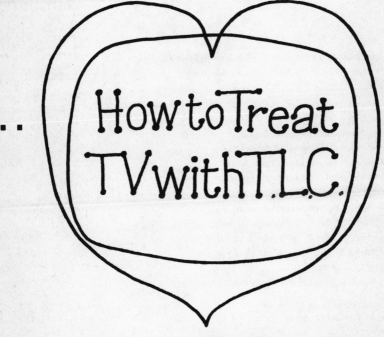

How to Treat TV with T.L.C.

EVELYN KAYE

with the cooperation of the American Academy of Pediatrics
illustrations by Edward Frascino
and additional designs by Richard Lyons and Charles Beier

BEACON PRESS   Boston

Copyright © 1979 by Action for Children's Television, Inc.

Illustrations © 1979 by Action for Children's

Television, Inc.

All royalties from the sale of this book will go to Action
for Children's Television

Beacon Press books are published under the auspices
of the Unitarian Universalist Association

Published simultaneously in Canada by
Fitzhenry & Whiteside Limited, Toronto

All rights reserved

Printed in the United States of America

(hardcover) 9 8 7 6 5 4 3 2 1
(paperback) 9 8 7 6 5 4 3 2 1

Library of Congress Cataloging in Publication Data

Action for Children's Television.
   The ACT guide to children's television.

   Bibliography: p.
   1. Television and children. 2. Television
programs for children—United States. I. Kaye,
Evelyn, 1937. II. American Academy of
Pediatrics. III. Title. IV. Guide to Children's
television.
HQ784.T4A3   791.45'5   78-53654
ISBN 0-8070-2366-3

WITH SPECIAL THANKS

—to Peggy Charren

—to those professionals working with children who care about television

—to those TV broadcasters who care about children

—to producers, writers, advertisers, journalists, and parents who have shared their advice and experiences

—to all the supporters and members of ACT who have shown their limitless encouragement for ACT's ideals

—and to my husband, Christopher Sarson, and two TV-watching children, Katrina and David, who started it all

The ACT Guide
to
Children's Television

The ACT Guide to Children's Television

or...

Revised Edition

Contents

Foreword   *Peggy Charren and Jean Johnson*   ix

Preface   How to Tame the TV Monster   *T. Berry Brazelton, M.D.*   xiii

Introduction   Who is Talking to Your Children?   *1*

Chapter 1   To View or Not to View   *7*

Chapter 2   Professional Opinions   *15*

Chapter 3   The Business of Broadcasting   *27*

Chapter 4   Children's TV Programming   *35*

Chapter 5   How to Treat TV with T.L.C.   *53*

Chapter 6   Television and the Classroom   *67*

Chapter 7   Violence and the FCC   *79*

Chapter 8   The Advertising Game—Gimme Gimme Gimme   *95*

Chapter 9   The Federal Trade Commission and Children's Advertising   *109*

Chapter 10   The Selling Game and How to Win It   *119*

Chapter 11   Children's Workbook   *129*

Chapter 12   What You Can Do   *149*

Appendix A   A Short Course in Broadcasting   *173*

Appendix B   Violence in Children's Television Programs   *177*

Appendix C   ACT Achievement Awards   *183*

Appendix D   Resource Directory   *Prepared by Jean Johnson*   *193*

Appendix E   Bibliography   *203*

Appendix F   ACTFACTS   *217*

Foreword

Peggy Charren, President, Action for Children's Television

Jean Johnson, Resource Director, Action for Children's Television

Few Americans gave it much thought in the early days. Modern technology had brought forth a new miracle. Television could bring the world into our living rooms, and what's more, the medium would bring us together. Families and friends, too often scattered among varying pursuits, would instead gather together to share an evening of television.

It may be that we have now come full circle. As television has proliferated, and as its profits have soared, so too have the pejoratives multiplied. Television is termed the "boob tube," the "idiot box," or the "vast wasteland." The medium which was to be the savior of the American family is now indicted as a cause of its disintegration. As the first television generation reaches maturity, our attitudes toward the medium, and our expectations of it, have changed markedly.

Ten years ago, Action for Children's Television began to question television's impact on its youngest viewers. Gathering expert testimony, ACT confirmed what most parents suspected: television was a major educator of American children, and too often, its lessons were poorly planned in terms of its youngest viewers. ACT took a hard look at the industry practices which placed the needs of broadcasters and advertisers above the needs of children, and ACT demanded change.

A decade of activity gives us cause for optimism. Programming and advertising practices have improved. Children and their families have a wider array of program choices than ever before. Whether they select from the diverse children's offerings on public television or choose among the quality specials on commercial stations, American families can, at least on occasion, view some of the best children's programming available anywhere. Even the Saturday morning cartoons are periodically enlivened by features such as CBS's new children's magazine, "30 Minutes," and ABC's "Short Story Specials."

Although children are still subjected to an unceasing barrage of commercials for highly sugared foods and poorly made toys, some of the worst abuses have been curtailed. Due to ACT's efforts, ads for vitamins and fireworks are no longer aimed directly at child audiences. Commercial time on children's programs has been reduced by 40 percent. And in 1978, the Federal Trade Commission opened a major investigation into children's advertising. In response to increasing concern over manipulative TV advertising practices, the Commission will consider banning all advertising directed to viewers under eight and eliminating commercials for highly sugared snack foods aimed at children under twelve.

The Commission's activities signal a welcome change in the attitudes and the actions of government regulatory agencies. Coupled with increasing recognition of the child audience by concerned decision-makers in both the broadcasting and the corporate communities, the FTC rule-making procedure could pave the way for significant and long-lasting change in children's broadcasting.

Programming and advertising reforms are, it must be recognized, only a partial solution. Meaningful improvement of a child's TV viewing experience also depends on the concern and commitment of the adults who know children best. Parents, teachers, physicians, child-care providers—all have a unique and significant role to play in teaching children to use television wisely. Educating young viewers to select programs and to watch them critically can make television a positive, rather than a negative, factor in children's lives.

There are those who would have us believe that the best television is no television, or that, as the pundits put it, the most intellectual thing we can say about television is that we don't own a set. But a total rejection of television in the 1970s is no more realistic than the overblown expectations of the

1950s. Television is neither the cause of all our problems nor the cure for all our ills. Television is no less and no more than what we make of it.

ACT's accomplishments assure us that persuasion and perseverance can promote meaningful changes in broadcast practices. Moreover, our experiences have convinced us that television can enrich and stimulate our children's lives. We hope that the *ACT Guide to Children's Television* will open the door to a greater understanding of television's impact on young viewers and provide a key to the very best use of television for children and their families.

Preface
How to Tame
the TV Monster
A Pediatrician's Advice [1]

T. Berry Brazelton, M.D.

For a long time we have known that television plays an important role in the lives of our children. But only within the last few years have we begun to understand how powerful its influence really is, and many of us are worried. Recognizing the problem is one thing; solving it is another.

As a parent and as a pediatrician, I think the situation is not hopeless—difficult, yes, but not hopeless. I think there are some positive steps we can take to control this monster medium. Before we get into practical things you can do, however, let me first sketch the basis of my concern about television—about what it is and what it does.

My uneasiness is related to my studies of newborn babies. When a baby is born he is thrust from a protective existence inside his mother's womb into a hostile world outside. And given the fact that his major job involves simply trying to achieve some kind of equilibrium between himself and his new world, it has always amazed me that he is able to interact with his environment in the sophisticated way he does.

From the moment of birth an infant is able to take in and process information. He has a set of powerful mechanisms that allow him to control his universe, that allow him to respond with true discrimination to the sights and sounds around him. Since he might otherwise be at the mercy of all the stimuli to which he is exposed, he has the capacity to shut out those he judges "inappropriate."

A good example of what I mean by this comes from studies my co-workers and I carried out on newborn infants. We exposed a group of quietly resting babies to a disturbing visual stimulus—a bright operating room light—placed twenty-four inches from their heads. The light was on for three seconds, then off for one minute. The sequence was repeated twenty times. Throughout the test the babies were monitored for changes in their heartbeat, respiration, and brain waves. The first time the babies were exposed to the light stimulus, they were visibly startled; however, the intensity of their reaction decreased rapidly after a few times. By the tenth stimulus there were no changes in behavior, heartbeat, or respiration. By the fifteenth stimulus, sleep patterns appeared on the electroencephalogram, although it was clear that their eyes were still taking in the light. After twenty stimuli the babies awoke from their "induced" sleep to scream and thrash about.

Our experiment demonstrated that a newborn certainly is not at the mercy of his environment. He has a marvelous mechanism, a shutdown device, for dealing with disturbing stimuli: he can tune them out and go into a sleeplike state.

But if we can imagine the amount of energy a newborn baby expends in managing this kind of shutdown—energy he could put to better use—we can see how expensive this mechanism becomes when it is at work all the time.

And if we can realize this, I think, we may be getting to some understanding of the way television works and the way it affects small children. For just like the operating room light, television creates an environment that assaults and overwhelms the child; he can respond to it only by bringing into play his shutdown mechanism and thus becomes more passive.

I have observed this in my own children and I have seen it in other people's children. As they sat in front of a television set that was blasting away, watching a film of horrors of rapidly varying kinds, the children were completely quiet. Nails bitten, thumbs in mouth, faces pale, bodies tense—they were "hooked." If anyone interrupted, tapped a child on the shoulder to break through his state of rapt attention, he almost always would start and might even break down in angry crying. If he was led away from the set, he often dissolved into a combative, screaming, wildly thrashing mass.

Sigmund Freud's daughter Anna, an eminent child analyst, once called such behavior the "disintegration of the ego." Indeed, it seemed that whatever ego the child had was being sorely tested at a time like that. And I think the intensity of the reaction is clear evidence of the energy the child is putting into television watching and the shock he experiences when his attention, locked onto the screen, is broken into.

What bothers me most about television is the passivity it forces on children—the passivity that requires all activity to be produced for them, not by them. This, I feel, must have a powerful influence on any child's capacity to handle his normal aggressive impulses.

By the time a child is five or six years old, his fantasies are already as violent as those in any horror movie adults might construct, and his sexual fantasies can match anything presented in a grade C movie. The violence and adult forms of sexuality displayed on television mobilize these fantasies together with all the fear and anxiety that go with them.

I feel that this is one of the grave dangers of all the violence and sexual activity to which children are exposed—not that children are taught anything new by it, but that it strikes at very primitive impulses and mobilizes them, but leaves children with no way to give healthy expression to them. It comes down to the fact that television gives a child two choices: he can actively suppress his feelings or he can ineffectually play them out.

No wonder, then, that a child comes away from a television set believing that physical violence is a perfectly acceptable form of self-expression.

When we adults watch a television program—or a movie, for that matter—we do not always respond to what we see at the very moment it is being presented. Particularly if the material is disturbing or otherwise provocative, we often avoid immediate confrontation with it. But at a later time—an hour or so afterward, perhaps even the next day—we think about what we have seen. We reflect on it and compare it with our own experiences and our own store of ideas. We make sense of it first and then decide whether it is true for us.

But a child can't bring this sort of control to what he sees on television because his intellectual development hasn't taken him that far. He can't delay his response until he has mulled it over and tested it in his mind; he can't go back to it later. He is hooked into the experience of the moment; he gives himself totally to what he is viewing. The sights and sounds coming from the television screen wash over him then and there, and he can't protect himself, as we can, with intellectual detachment. He is forced to be a passive receiver.

In this sense, watching television for a child is totally different from reading—which might seem to be a similar passive activity. First of all, when a young child is reading he is putting into operation a skill he has newly acquired, and this in itself requires active participation on his part. As he struggles over each syllable, each word, he tries to relate it to other syllables and words, to other ideas he has learned. Though physically undemanding, reading requires a child to be mentally alert, to think, to bring to it something of himself.

And then, of course, the material presented in children's books is totally different from the kind that fills the television screen. Usually there is nothing so threatening, nothing so overwhelming, nothing so likely to stir up a child's unconscious fantasies. The authors and editors of children's literature are very scrupulous about this today. They are concerned about issues in child development: they are concerned about the age appropriateness of the material they publish, and often indicate that a book is recommended for children in a certain age bracket.

But this is not true for television, which for the most part does not take into account differences in age and in sensitivity among its young viewers. Adventure movies, even cartoons, may contain a level of violence and brutality that may not faze a seven- or eight-year-old, because at that age children can make a clearer distinction between what is real and true to life and what is not. But for a three- or four-year-old, such distinctions are not possible. Younger children may watch a cartoon show and come away disturbed and upset, though an adult—or an older child, for that matter—would consider it totally harmless. They cannot understand why Tom keeps hitting Jerry; they worry about how much it hurts. As a result, they themselves feel confused and vulnerable.

Still, even though we have to face the fact that television is not the best medium for a child to be exposed to, it does have an undeniable importance in the world today. From all the evidence it looks as if it is going to be around for a very long time, and we simply have to come to terms with it. But this does *not* mean that we as parents must throw up our hands in dismay and resignation. There are a few outstanding television programs for children, which means that "quality" is possible—if we demand it. Further, we *can* take some steps now to control what and how much television our children watch.

So now let's talk about what is right with television. The first time I was exposed to such programs as "Sesame Street," "Mister Rogers' Neighborhood," and, more recently, "The Electric Company," I began to be aware of the real potential for good that television programs can provide. Instead of being overwhelming, depleting, passive experiences, these programs demonstrated that small children could have warming times and learn exciting things—about their world and about themselves—in a period of television watching.

I first became aware of Mister Rogers when one of my four-year-old patients quoted him during his entire examination in my office. He was a boy who had been frightened of me on previous visits but was trying hard to master his anxiety this time. After I applied the cold stethoscope to his chest he nodded and said, "Just like Mister Rogers." When I used the earpiece, he winced but allowed it, saying, "Just like Mister Rogers." Before his shot he said, "Mister Rogers said it was okay for kids my age to cry for a shot. Do you think it is, Dr. Brazelton?"

Not to be outdone by this mythical Mister Rogers, I said, "Of course it is, Dan. And you know what? If you look the other way and let out a yell when I do it, it won't even hurt too much." These maneuvers worked to distract him. He yelled for a minute after the shot, then stopped and with a straight face said, "You're almost as good for kids as Mister Rogers."

By this time I wanted very much to congratulate a man who could prepare a child for a frightening experience by using a television program. By demonstrating what might happen on a visit to the doctor and by giving suggestions about how to face up to the anxiety and the pain it might bring, he had helped this boy through an ordeal and given him a chance to be proud of himself.

"Sesame Street" was literally shoved down my throat day after day by one three-year-old after another who read the letters from my eye chart with the musical phrase appropriate to each letter. I have watched "Sesame Street" myself, and I can see what a powerful teaching medium it is.

I do not feel that all the programs children watch must be "learning" experiences. Children really need to relax after a day in school; they must have some "throwaway" time. And I think they would find it in other ways—in comic books, for example— even if we could construct enough educational programs to fill the prime-time hours.

But it does seem that children really might prefer to be offered "good" and thoughtful programs for their selection. This is pointed up by the enormous number who watch repeats of "Sesame Street" or of "Mister Rogers' Neighborhood," who will cut off a war drama or a stirring love story their parents are watching to tune in to these repeats. My children say, "But, Dad, these programs are for *me*."

I feel that all you parents should try to acquaint yourselves with the programs that are being offered in your area, and then you can play an active part in your child's television viewing. Every Sunday or Monday, for example, you and your child could sit down with a guide to the week's shows and discuss them together. For each day select one or two programs that you both agree would be entertaining and worthwhile. If your child insists on something you don't think is suitable, gently but firmly discuss your reasons with him.

You could also make your selections on a daily basis, gearing your choices around the day's events and your child's mood. For a quiet day, he might need a soothing storyteller or a visit with Mister Rogers. For a learning day, "Sesame Street" or "The Electric Company" might be more appropriate. But whichever method you decide to use, after the program follow up with a discussion about what went on and an assessment of its quality. In this way you can make the experience a deeper and more meaningful one for your child.

Ideally, of course, it would be best if you could actually be there with your child and watch the program along with him, because your presence and obvious concern will give a deeper and more human dimension to what is essentially an isolating experience. Perhaps you could see to it that you are in on at least one or two full programs per week. I realize that it is not always possible for a busy parent to do this, but I would urge you at least to try to be available during these times. Let your child know in advance that if he wants you for any reason—because he is disturbed by something he is watching, because he wants something explained, because he just needs you there with him—you'll certainly come. When and if this does happen, sit down and *listen* to him, trying to understand the concerns of his that have been stirred up.

Perhaps you might also think about the ways in which you can use television as a positive and cementing force within your family. For example, most mothers need a baby sitter at certain times of the day. They need the relief from demands of housekeeping and child rearing, the time to prepare the evening meal, an organizing force to bring children down from the exciting experiences of the day to a more relaxed, comfortable state. Appropriate programs could help to do this *and* provide children with a worthwhile experience. Programs that bring all the members of the household together after supper can be an opportunity for valuable interaction—for example, word games or guessing games in which all ages can participate actively *as a family.*

There is just one more point I would like to make. I believe one hour a day is the maximum amount of time a child up to the age of five or six can spend in front of a television set before he begins to show the signs of depletion and exhaustion that I mentioned earlier. But parents, in particular mothers, must always be on the lookout for the symptoms. Whenever they appear you can be certain that your child has had too much, and you must reduce the television-watching time accordingly.

In attempting to outline some of the problems television causes and in trying to give some ways of coping with them, I am not suggesting that we eliminate television altogether—I certainly am not that much of an ostrich. But I would urge all of us who are parents to take a more active role in this part of our children's lives. We must replace the almost total lack of control that exists today with individual choice, with the freedom to decide upon or to refuse a program. This kind of active participation on the part of the parent, as well as the child, may begin to make television the valuable experience it should be.

*   *   *

In the past few years, there has been more research and far more concern in the area of television programming designed for children. *The ACT Guide to Children's Television* is the prime example of a new awareness of the need of parents for information about the television that their children may see. One of the best starting places for a concerned family would be to read this book, and to experiment with the many viewing suggestions it contains. It can be the first step to active involvement in the viewing experiences of our children.

NOTE

[1] Reprinted from *Redbook* magazine, where Dr. Brazelton is Contributing Editor.

The ACT Guide
to
Children's Television

Introduction
Who is Talking to Your Children?

The room is half-darkened. In the corner the television shows an animated cartoon of a large animal chasing two smaller animals. Loud music accompanies the chase.

The screen then shows two figures from "The Flintstones" cartoon demonstrating the contents of a box of cereal. "If you put sweet Pebbles in your mouth, you won't have rocks in your head." There is rock music and the animated characters dance around. Next on the screen is a man walking up slowly behind a woman. He catches her by the throat and starts to strangle her. A tense voice urges: "Watch 'The Terror of the Underworld' on Adult Movies tonight at eleven on this station." With an echoing scream the woman fades away. The picture of the animal chase then reappears and a voice says: "Now back to 'Kimba.'"

A young boy sits sprawled on a chair watching the screen. He is chewing gum and looks mesmerized. Suddenly a woman comes into the room. "Good grief, what are you doing sitting in here? I thought you were outside riding your bike. Turn that thing off and go outside; it's a beautiful day."

The boy doesn't move, doesn't seem to have heard her. She goes to the TV and turns it off. He stretches, twists, yawns. "Now go outside," she says firmly. "That's enough TV for now." The boy wanders out of the room, mumbling, "I don't want to go out."

The woman watches him go. Did I do the right thing, she wonders. He wasn't bothering anyone. He had played outside earlier anyway. Maybe he'd have a fight with his brother now.

1

Parents today have a visitor in their homes. It produces a variety of reactions and can be found in over 97 percent of American households. The visitor is television and it has been here since the 1950s. Many adults feel a certain amount of guilt about watching television. They think that it is less worthwhile than reading a book or clearing up the yard. This is partly because of their ambivalence about the programs themselves. While we declare publicly that it is essential to have many regular news and cultural programs on TV, it is much easier to turn the dial to the movie rerun or the comedy hour which is inane but relaxing. There is also an incredible deluge of advertising that accompanies television programs, coloring our attitudes and speech to such an extent that advertising slogans become national catch phrases.

Although parents learn to cope with their own feelings about television, they are often confused about their children's viewing attitudes. Most people over thirty-one can remember a time before television took over as the mass entertainer. But for young children and adolescents life without television is as unthinkable as life without electricity or cars or the sky.

Television fascinates many children, often more than radio, records, or books. While parents report that some children are bored by watching and voluntarily seek out other activities, most will sit passively for hours absorbing whatever images move across the screen and the jumble of music, words, programs, and ads that make up a TV soundtrack. According to John Condry, professor of human development and family studies at Cornell University:

"Our understanding of the impact of this medium has lagged far behind its commercial success. We have only recently become aware of the changes it has brought about in the nature of politics, the entertainment industry, and the dissemination of news. Whether these changes will be, in the long run, good or bad is still to be determined. Yet the changes television brings to these and other areas of American life may prove trivial compared to its potential effect upon the lives of children."[1]

What can parents do to cope with TV and to help their children live with this new medium? The ACT Guide to Children's

Television incorporates the experience of many parents, from different parts of the country and different ways of life, including those involved with the work of Action for Children's Television (ACT). We welcome your comments, ideas, and suggestions.

HOW MUCH DO YOU KNOW ABOUT CHILDREN'S TELEVISION?

Before you turn to Chapter 1, test your knowledge of children's television with the following quiz. Score yourself. If you get less than 100 percent, read on. There is more you should know about children's TV.

1. By the time a child has finished high school, he has spent 11,000 hours in classrooms. How many hours were spent watching television during those years?
   2,000 hours   10,000 hours   15,000 hours
   25,000 hours

drawing by Rob Chalfen

2. Is there any relationship between televised violence and aggressive behavior in children?
definitely yes   definitely no   probably yes
probably no

3. Which network runs children's programs with no commercials?
ABC   CBS   PBS   NBC

4. Which are the two most commonly advertised products on programs designed for children (Circle two):
toothpaste   fish   milk   apples   candy   cookies
toys   snack foods   cheese   cereals   lettuce
vitamin pills   soap   peanut butter   carrots   juice

5. Food is often advertised on Saturday morning children's TV. What percentage of the food ads are for nutritious foods such as fruit, vegetables, meat, bread, or milk?
4 percent   5 percent   12 percent   28 percent

6. Children's programs broadcast during the weekdays before 6:00 P.M. contain more minutes of advertising than programs broadcast during adult prime time.
True   False

7. The National Association of Broadcasters' *Television Code* states: "Children shall not be directed to purchase or to ask a parent or other adult to buy a product or service for them." Who enforces the code?
a special board   the FCC   TV stations   the police

8. How many network programs especially designed for young children are aired Monday through Friday in the daytime on commercial television?
One   Three   Seven   Fifteen

9. Public television has provided many children's programs. Which of the following uses only material sent in by child viewers as the basis for subsequent programs?
"Sesame Street"   "Electric Company"   "ZOOM"
"Mister Rogers' Neighborhood"   "Carrascolendas"
"Villa Alegre"   "REBOP"   "Once upon a Classic"
"Inside/Out"

10. Hosts of programs and cartoon characters in children's shows are forbidden to introduce or present any commercials.

True   False

QUIZ ANSWERS

1. 15,000 hours—and this is based on a conservative average figure, so that many children watch much more.

2. Definitely yes; the hearings on the 1971 Surgeon General's investigation into violence showed that there were clear indications that watching violent TV had some effect on children.

3. PBS, the Public Broadcasting System.

4. Any of the following: cereals, snack foods, toys, candy, cookies.

5. Less than 4 percent of the ads for food on Saturday morning TV are for nutritious foods, such as fruit, vegetables, or bread.

6. True. Weekday children's programs contain twelve minutes of non-program material per hour. Adult prime time contains only nine and a half minutes per hour.

7. No one enforces the NAB *Television Code.* It is voluntary. Indeed, the Westinghouse group of stations withdrew from the code because it felt the standards were too low.

8. One! "Captain Kangaroo" is the only daily daytime program specially designed for children on commercial television.

9. "ZOOM," produced by WGBH-TV, Boston, is made up entirely of jokes, stories, plays, songs, and poems sent in by young viewers and presented by seven children.

10. True. The NAB code, in response to public pressure, has ruled that hosts on children's programs cannot sell products or present commercials.

NOTE

[1] *Action for Children's Television* (New York: 1971), pp. 61–62.

To View or Not to View

The A. C. Nielsen Company is a major source of statistics about TV viewing habits, and network executives scrutinize its ratings carefully whenever they appear.

Children are measured in two groups, two- to five-year-olds and six- to eleven-year olds, and the amount they watch influences the amount the family unit watches. Nielsen finds that families with young children have the set on more frequently than families with older children or no children.

A table compiled by the Nielsen Company (Figure 1) summarizes some important statistics about children's TV viewing.

WHAT'S YOUR TOTAL?

Parents who are starting to wonder about television and its effects on their children might like to check TV watching for a week by jotting down how many hours their own children watch, or asking their children to do it themselves (see "Children's Workbook," p. 129). Many parents may be surprised to discover how much time their children actually spend in front of the TV. Other parents may find that TV is only one activity within a week that is full of other things to do. And some parents who keep the set on all day as a background to other activities may not consider this "viewing" in the strict sense of the word. Each family has its own feelings about television and it is important to make sure that you feel comfortable about the kind of viewing that your children do. But first find out.

WEEKLY VIEWING ACTIVITY FOR MEN, WOMEN, TEENS AND CHILDREN[1] *

NIELSEN ESTIMATES
NTI/NAC AUDIENCE DEMOGRAPHICS REPORT
NOVEMBER 1976

	MON.-SUN. 7:30-11PM	MON.-SUN. 4:30-7:30PM	MON.-FRI. 7AM-4:30PM	SAT.-SUN. 7AM-4:30PM	MON.-SUN. 11PM-7AM	HOURS/MINS. PER WEEK
DISTRIBUTION OF HOURS IN WEEK	15%	13%	28%	11%	33%	168:00
TOTAL PERSONS	38%	23%	18%	10%	11%	28:41
WOMEN 18–24	34%	20%	24%	14%	8%	30:05
WOMEN 25–54	39%	19%	22%	7%	13%	32:14
WOMEN 55+	36%	23%	25%	6%	10%	35:23
MEN 18–24	40%	21%	8%	18%	13%	21:21
MEN 25–54	43%	21%	8%	11%	17%	26:38
MEN 55+	38%	16%	25%	11%	10%	32:40
FEMALE TEENS	40%	26%	15%	12%	7%	21:05
MALE TEENS	40%	25%	11%	14%	10%	22:35
CHILDREN 6–11	35%	29%	18%	14%	4%	26:40
CHILDREN 2–5	24%	28%	29%	17%	2%	29:05

*Reprinted from *Nielsen Television 1977* by permission of A. C. Nielsen Company.

Figure 1

HOW TO REGULATE TV VIEWING

Parents have different ways of regulating TV viewing in their families. You can choose from a range of parent-tested methods if you decide that your child is watching too much television.

1. No television viewing at all; it is an adult occupation. Some parents of very young children feel that this is an essential rule.
2. Limiting number of hours for viewing TV. It could be an hour a day on school days, perhaps more on weekends. Or a total number of hours each week.
3. No viewing until homework or chores are completed, or during specific times. Some parents find it helps to keep the set off during meal times, music practice times, or early morning hours before school.
4. Viewing only on weekends, not during the week.
5. No viewing of commercial television programs, only public (non-commercial) programs.
6. Selecting programs in advance from television listings and permitting the set to be on only at those times.
7. Viewing only in bad weather when children cannot play outside. This is easier in climates with mild winters or in areas where children have adequate play space outside.
8. Unlimited viewing at any time. Parents who choose this method believe that it is all right for the child to decide what he or she wants to watch without any parental guidance.

Many parents find it helpful to discuss television viewing with older children and to talk to them about the kind of rules that they would find acceptable. Sometimes children appreciate a firm stand on viewing and welcome knowing where the boundaries are. It is wise to tell your children in advance of any regulations that you set, so that they know what is going to happen. With young children, there may be noisy complaints when you first implement certain rules and turn the set off to comply with the limits.

Home Situation and TV

The amount of television a child watches often depends on her or his particular situation at home. Children alone at home with a parent may start watching television because there is little else provided for them to do. If no older brothers and sisters or friends are around, television may be a substitute. But often parents can wean children from the set by providing simple, creative toys or activities for them to become involved in. A morning spent mixing flour and water for play dough will make most children happier than watching the game shows and old movies which many TV stations run in the early part of the day. For older children, television may be an escape if they are timid about playing with new friends or when they are having a difficult time in a neighborhood situation. Parents can often help by talking to their children about excessive TV watching. They can also set up enjoyable outings or local activities involving neighbors.

Unusual situations, such as moving or receiving unexpected visitors, or times of stress, such as sickness or the extended absence of a parent, may mean that parents have less time to spend with their child, who is left to watch television. When the regular routine is interrupted, it is sometimes difficult to stop the temporary increase in viewing after the situation returns to normal. It is important for children to know, however, that in periods of stress and confusion they *can* turn to their parents for the time and attention that they need, rather than to the television set.

Don't Abandon a Child to the Set!

Leaving a young child alone in a room with a television set is not recommended. Parents then have no idea what the children are watching and are allowing them to make many unwise viewing decisions. If the children are worried or frightened about something they see, they have nobody to turn to for comfort.

Life Without Television

A few families feel that their lives are simplified if they just don't have a TV set in the house. Often there are major news stories about families who have "given up television." However, the gesture is only symbolic in many ways. Television is around us everywhere. There's a TV set in 97 percent of American homes. Children whose parents ban TV at home can watch it at friends' homes, at school, in stores. There is practically no way that a child in twentieth-century America can grow up without being exposed to television at some point.

Since television is pervasive, and probably here to stay, it's important for parents to realize that the best thing they can do is help their children be selective about viewing. If the parent is concerned about programming, then it is vital that children learn to check the listings before turning on the set. If the parent is concerned about commercialism, it's clear that children must learn to choose the noncommercial public channel.

What's more, there is a wide range of outstanding programs that can be highly beneficial for children. Reading comics or badly written adventure stories may be far less enlightening than watching a *National Geographic* special or a superb dramatization such as "Roots." Just because it's in print doesn't automatically give it cultural superiority; there's as much badly written print around as there is poor quality television.

Judicious choice and careful reading of program listings can give parents and children a reasonably good selection of programs over the year, because children's programming has changed in the last decade. The arrival of "Sesame Street" and the other noncommercial programs on public broadcasting has greatly altered the face of children's television. And in response to that success and to public pressure, commercial television has also created some exciting new series for children. Given television's ability to offer, at least intermittently, stimulating programs for children and adults, few families seem willing to eliminate television entirely.

Several years ago, researchers paid families to give up television for a year. The major result was that by the end of the year, not a single family had stayed with the project. For a variety of reasons—wanting to watch the news, needing relaxation, watching movies, finding the long winter evenings impossible—the families one by one withdrew and asked for their TV sets back.

Whether we like it or not, television is an integral part of our modern lives. Those in their forties are the last generation to remember a time "before television." The best thing we can do for our children is help them to understand this modern invention and to use it to enhance and enrich rather than invade and overwhelm their lives.

SOME QUESTIONS PARENTS ASK

Question: Children spend all day in school learning. Why can't they be allowed to relax and enjoy TV in the afternoons and on weekends?

Answer: They certainly can, but for a child, learning and entertainment are not totally separate. Children learn from everything they see and do. They learn from an outdated animated cartoon, and from a program labeled "educational." Some parents have found that watching certain kinds of TV programs is not at all relaxing for their children, but instead provokes tension and irritability. Pediatricians and others who work with children have noted the same syndrome. Dr. Aletha Huston Stein, in her article "Mass Media and Young Children's Development," in the *Yearbook of the National Society for the Study of Education* (1972), states:

"Children apparently react to media more intensely than adults. More important, they often interpret a plot differently and, as a result, respond emotionally to different aspects of its content."[2]

Her studies also found that media presentations involving violence, danger, conflict, and tragedy stimulate immediate emotional reactions. Another study found that children watching an aggressive cartoon exhibited more signs of anxiety than those watching a nonaggressive cartoon.[3]

It is important for parents to know which programs make their children feel good and which don't. Broadcasters, on the other hand, should assume the responsibility for providing as varied a range of programs for children as possible, so that the children will have a real choice in what they can watch.

Question: I tried setting some limits on what my children watched but it caused such arguments that I wonder if it's worth it.

Answer: It is hard to set rules in any family. But it is important to realize that young children think that adults control everything in the home and presume that what comes over the television is also there with parental approval. You can show your concern for your children by setting limits, so that they will know how you feel about television. Children often appreciate rules once they know you mean what you say and as long as the rules are applied consistently.

NOTES

[1] A. C. Nielsen Company, *Nielsen Television 1977* (New York: A. C. Nielsen Company, 1977), p. 10.
[2] P. 18.
[3] David L. Lange, Robert K. Baker, and Sandra J. Ball, *Mass Media and Violence* (Washington, D.C.: 1969).

Professional Opinions

Many professionals who work with children daily—teachers, pediatricians, child psychiatrists—are aware of the amount of television children watch. Their comments echo the concerns of parents across the country. Although there is no general agreement among experts about whether watching TV is good or bad for children, many are concerned about its effects, both the physical effects of sitting passively for long periods of time and the emotional effects of the kinds of programs watched. Dr. Richard Granger, associate professor of clinical pediatrics at the Yale University Child Study Center, has stated:

We have, as a nation, acted as though no body of knowledge about the developmental needs and pitfalls of childhood existed. If this is so for a society at large, why pick on television in particular? A prime reason is that for a large number of children, television is society at large. Through its powerfully combined audio and visual impact delivered directly into the child's home, it is the face of the adult world, the reflection of society.[1]

In 1971, the American Academy of Pediatrics, representing 12,000 pediatricians in the United States, Canada, and Latin America, wrote to the Federal Communications Commission:

We are naturally concerned with television programing for our children, since this communications medium today affects so significantly the learning and behavioral habits of children. We feel it is essential that commercial broadcasters recognize their responsibility to program for the child audience. . . . We urge that at least half of all prime time be especially constructed with the best interests of children in mind.

15

Bernice Miller, an educator and one of the founders of the New School, an experimental elementary school for black children in Roxbury, Massachusetts, has voiced a strong criticism of racism on current children's TV:

One, television is misused. Two, it perpetuates racial prejudice in a racist society. Three, it has a great potential which we have not as yet explored. And four, educators ought to get into the fight, particularly teachers, because if television is ever developed as a learning device it is going to be the teacher who is still going to be in constant contact with the child.[2]

And Dr. Carolyn Block, director of children's services, Westside Community Mental Health Center in San Francisco, California, said at a 1975 ACT symposium:

It is in the areas of social behavior, social expectations, and social norms that blacks and other minority children are often disserved by television . . . if one takes a look at present black programming, it is easy to conclude that all black people are funny and/or stupid. They sing, dance, talk tough, play sports, and dress well. Black television characterizations, particularly in television series, rarely depict true dominance and leadership, affection, or success in prestigious occupations. In short, black characters are rarely seen as competent, well-functioning human beings who are capable of controlling and affecting their own lives in serious ways.

WHAT ELSE ARE CHILDREN LEARNING?

Children absorb a great many messages from their television viewing, and often these are much more subtle than the simple plot and counterplot.

One area of concern to many professionals who work with children is the role models that children see on the screen. For example, statistics show that more and more women are now working full time. Yet television situation comedies and commercials continue to show women in stereotypical homemaker roles with no more pressing problems on their minds than how to get the stains out of a pair of jeans.

The U.S. Civil Rights Commission, in a 181-page report, entitled *Window Dressing on the Set* and released in October 1977, makes a strong case for improved minority hiring practices at local TV stations, and comments on stereotyping in TV shows.

Helen Franzwa, project director of the report, is quoted:

We're suggesting that these characters are role models whether anyone wants them to be or not. People learn from them; they get a lot of information about certain kinds of groups from what they see on television. Children develop lots of ideas about minorities from television, especially if they don't have actual contact with them. All we're really saying is, it has an impact.

Moreover, the report continues, "television's portrayal of women and minorities and the potential impact of these portrayals are issues of critical importance to the American society."

Minorities on programs designed for children are as stereotyped and misrepresented as they often are on adult programs. In a pilot study carried out for ACT by Black Efforts for Soul in Television (BEST) in Washington, D.C., children's Saturday morning programs were analyzed for racial and nonwhite emphasis. The study found that non-American and nonwhite cultures were referred to negatively almost every time they were mentioned, and that black and other minority characters made up only a small percentage of characters: 7 percent in the case of blacks and 2 percent for other minorities.

The analysis found that the subject of race was never mentioned or discussed, and that even in shows with black stars or characters, blacks interacted only with white characters in a white community. Occasional black leaders had white co-leaders, but most shows had white leaders. All four references to American Indians were derogatory.

In 1975 Dr. F. Earle Barcus classified 405 program characters shown in afterschool hours in ten cities, and found that 74 percent were male, 96 percent were white, 3 percent were black and 1 percent were other identifiable minorities.

He also found, after examining more than 200 hours of programs broadcast between 3:00 and 6:00 P.M. on sixty-eight independent stations, that there was a practice "of relabeling programs produced for prime time TV as children's television." Ads during these programs were mainly aimed at children.[3]

An evaluation of network programming entitled "The New Children's Television: A Profile of the 1974–75 Season," conducted by the Media Action Research Center, revealed that "females and children of black, Hispanic, Indian, Oriental, and other minority groups are still without adequate representation, and see almost no models with whom they can identify."

At the very least, television helps to socialize a new generation of children into an already existing pattern. Aimee Dorr Leifer, Neal J. Gordon, and Sherryl Browne Graves commented in an article in the *Harvard Educational Review:*

To the extent that television does not reflect reality, it socializes children into a fictitious social system, where criminals are always caught, minorities and the elderly are rarely seen, guilty people always break down under a good lawyer's barrage of questions, problems are solved in an hour, and things usually work out for the best.[4]

Television's curriculum on sex roles begins early. Rita Dohrmann, professor of sociology at Drake University, Des Moines, Iowa, examined 390 characters from children's programs such as "Sesame Street," "Electric Company," "Mister Rogers' Neighborhood," and "Captain Kangaroo." The characters were analyzed for "active mastery" roles and "passive dependent" behavior.

About two-thirds of incidents were active, the rest passive. Men and boys were "more than twice as likely to exhibit masterful behavior than passive dependent ones," while girls were less likely to have active roles.

Males got the best examples in learning "to lead others, to solve problems, to have one's self-confidence boosted by reward, to have the satisfaction of helping others and to show self-control."

Dohrmann found that girls' educational patterns were exactly opposite: "As a whole, they are more likely to follow than lead, to praise rather than be rewarded, to be fearful seekers of protection rather than self-determined individuals. Jobs are almost exclusively held by males, even though 40 percent of the employees in the United States are women.

"Males compose 100 percent of the lead characters—the moderators who serve as authority figures—and dominate the ranks of major characters as well," Dohrmann states. Her concern is that children exposed to these concepts from an early age will learn that boys can lead and solve problems while girls can be dominated by male power. She adds: "I am especially concerned with these particular programs because they are often cited as the best and brightest of children's television fare."[5] Moreover, in the 1974–75 study of Saturday morning children's TV programs, the Media Action Research Center (Dr. Robert Liebert, Susan Harvey, and Rita Poulos) found that 72 percent of all human roles were assigned to males.

Characters in toy ads were usually identified by sex roles, girls playing with dolls and boys with cars. Since children will have seen 350,000 commercials and 15,000 hours of television by the time they are eighteen, it is obviously important to examine the influence of the sex stereotypes to which they have been exposed in both programs and commercials. Letty Cottin Pogrebin, a writer and editor, said in a speech at Yale University in 1972:

Check out the cartoons, like "The Flintstones," and sitcoms like " I Love Lucy" and see how kids learn that women are scheming, brainless, deceptive and frivolous, that women control their men through devious comic plots but they never possess power or dignity, that men are said to be problem solvers, workers in the world outside the home, brave and courageous when called upon. So it is okay occasionally to portray them as bunglers around the house. Consider also occupational unreality. Over 30 million American women work, and nearly half of all married women have jobs outside the home. Yet we cannot find any female character in children's shows or situation comedies who is a working wife or mother—married and working.[6]

The National Organization for Women has a media committee which is presently involved in research in this area.

Other studies have been concerned with the concepts of the elderly that children absorb from TV, concepts that promote unrealistic ideas of what elderly people can do and what they are like. There have been efforts by groups like the Gray Panthers to diversify some of the portrayals of older Americans on television, and to persuade writers and producers to discourage comedians like Carol Burnett or Johnny Carson from depicting ridiculous old characters in their shows. However, these concerns are not specifically directed at children's programming, but affect the whole spectrum of television today.

Social Relationships On Programs

The types of characters on a program and their relationships with each other are often an indication of whether or not the program is constructive. Many shows are built around a simple conflict situation, which is resolved in the last two minutes.

The major problem in almost all shows is the existence of a power differential. There is somebody who is stronger or bigger or meaner or smarter than somebody else. The conflict presented is how to redress or diminish or eliminate that differential. This is a real problem for children, and for adults too. What is striking is the limited range of solutions proposed. You can use magic or cunning or cheating. It is recognized immediately that the hero figure must be successful at the end. No problems are without solutions. But rarely do characters use thoughtfulness, cooperation, or reason to solve them.

Many of the family situation series have little relation to the real life problems of growing children. Family relationships are almost always simplistic stereotypes. Children certainly learn character traits from such series, but rarely ones adaptable to the realities of conflict and disharmony which sometimes occur in real families. One of the entries in the diary of the young man who shot Governor Wallace in 1972 expressed the wish that his family "could be like those happy families on television." Do children understand that no families are like those "ideal" families on television?

In judging social relationships on television programs, parents must decide if they are ones they would want to see their children imitate and admire. If not, it may be simpler to stop your children from watching such programs than to argue constantly about values with which you do not agree.

Reality and Fantasy

Professionals who work with young children stress that one of the most important lessons a young child must learn is to distinguish between reality and fantasy. Dr. Albert Solnit, Sterling Professor of Pediatrics and Psychiatry and director of the Yale Child Study Center, has said:

Children under the age of six are more vulnerable to being confused because their sense of reality, their ability to use logic, their ability to use what we call orderly causal thinking is not as available to them developmentally until they are about six or seven. Under six or seven, and especially under the age of four, the very strong built-in capacity for explaining things by magical thinking, by the sense of the power of magical feeling, will make them more vulnerable to such confusion.[7]

When young children meet fantasy in books, they are usually with a sympathetic adult who is reading to them. If the fantasy becomes too frightening or confusing, the child can stop the adult and ask questions, or simply cuddle up close and enjoy "being scared." Children know that they can control the situation. Since young children generally cannot read fluently, the hobgoblins and giants of fairy stories come to them through the intermediary of an adult, at least until they are of school age and old enough to handle them.

But this is not the case with television. Children have no control over the program on the screen in front of them and they cannot stop it at a scary point and ask a question. For many children, television is the real world. When one nursery school teacher asked a young child: "Are Batman and Robin real or pretend?" he replied firmly: "Oh no, they're really real."

Children are often left to cope with a bewildering quantity of confusing information even during commercial breaks. In a pilot study, a TV commercial for a children's game called "The Secret of the Missing Mummy" was shown to a group of preschool children, followed by a few simple questions about what the commercial showed. Many of the young children were very disturbed by the commercial because they assumed that it referred to their own mother and indicated that she was missing. When asked why the Mummy was missing, one child replied: "Because she is making peanut butter and jelly sandwiches." Parents can help young children by watching with them, explaining things, and being ready to answer questions. Older brothers and sisters can sometimes also be helpful in this manner.

DISPLACEMENT?

Child professionals often point out that their major criticism of television is that it displaces other activities. A child who spends three hours one afternoon sitting in front of a television set is not spending those three hours doing other things. One pediatrician commented: "For very young children this can be a great loss because there are so many things that preschoolers need to try out and experiment with in these formative years. If young children do not have opportunities to test out experiences and learn about different materials and situations as well as about human relationships, they cannot have this time over again if it's spent in front of a TV set." For this reason, many pediatricians do not recommend leaving a baby or young child in front of the television for long periods of time, and urge parents to be aware of how much TV their young children are watching.

The National Child Research Center in Washington, D.C.,

was also critical in its 1971 filing with the FCC. "Television represses children's innate tendencies because it requires passive rather than active involvement, and activity not passivity is necessary for children's full healthful development."

Nursery school teachers know that young children need to learn by doing a variety of things. A good nursery or preschool will provide building blocks, puzzles, vessels to fill and empty, open and shut. There will be materials to mess with like water, play dough, clay, and paint, and dolls and animals for children to spank, wash, dry, dress, soothe, and cuddle. When young children spend a great deal of their time watching television, they lose an irreplaceable opportunity to learn the essential tasks for their age.

Dorothy Cohen, educator and author, reported that nursery school teachers are noticing a difference in the quality of children's play depending on the amount of television they see. "Teacher feedback in the primary grades shows that they are finding strong resistance among children not only to reading but to exerting any kind of effort. Something is happening to children in their ability to do."[8]

Dr. Lee Salk, in his column in *McCall's* magazine in December 1972, was more positive about children's television—in moderation:

Too much television is bad for a child—and for that matter, too much of anything is bad for anybody.

I must say that I think that many children are inadvertently forced into bad TV habits by their parents. When a parent wants some time alone or has been overburdened by a curious and enthusiastic child, it is too easy to say "Why don't you go and watch TV for a while?" Some parents offer extended viewing hours as a reward, others take it away as punishment. And so the importance of television is enhanced.

I do feel, however, that television has some fascinating programs to offer; but as with all other forms of entertainment, it is necessary for a parent to provide guidelines. If children see adults watching indiscriminately for hours, it is hard for them to see why they cannot do the same.

I think that a parent should help a child select programs that are emotionally and intellectually stimulating, and then be firm in limiting viewing to these. It is also far easier to divert a child with an interesting book or hobby than it is to turn off the TV and offer no alternative at all.[9]

Parents who turn off the set often find that children discover something else to do. Nature abhors a vacuum, and once children accept the idea that television cannot be constantly on when they are at home, they will find other ways to amuse themselves.

But Dr. Sherryl Graves of New York University says that research shows that too often "parents make very little attempt to regulate TV viewing, not because they don't care about their children, but because of an intense feeling of helplessness. . . . Many parents were at a total loss for what they would do with their children if they didn't have television there to keep them quiet and keep them off the streets."

One mother living in a large city commented: "I feel more comfortable knowing the two boys are indoors watching television than out on the streets getting into trouble—it's safer inside for them."

EXPANDING TELEVISION VIEWING

Television can be used as a springboard for other educational experiences.

Dr. Rosemary Potter, a Miami educator, has been talking with teachers about how to use TV constructively. What she does with her own nine-year-old twins is to associate programs with books. If they are going to watch a Jacques Cousteau special on uncovering a Spanish galleon, she brings books about the sea and old ships into the house, and finds that the children become as excited about reading *Treasure Island* as they were about watching Cousteau.

She discourages the idea of more than one TV set "so that a kid won't be off in a room some place watching something for hours and you won't know what's happening."[10]

The actual physical dangers of watching television can be more easily pinpointed and prevented. There may be some radiation from some color TV sets, and manufacturers advise sitting a specific distance from the set in order to avoid any danger. It is best to read carefully the instructions for your new set. The American Optometric Association has studied the effect of

TV viewing on the eyes and has prepared a pamphlet, "To View or Not to View,"[11] which states:

When properly installed and viewed, television is not harmful to the eyes or to vision. There is, normally, much less focus strain involved in viewing television than in doing close work such as reading or sewing. However, close concentration on the television screen over an excessive period of time may result in general fatigue. The AOA suggests that it is better not to sit too close to the screen, and recommends a distance of at least five times the width of the picture.

Their other recommendations include not watching in a completely dark room, not wearing sunglasses when watching, and not placing the TV set where there will be glare or reflections from lights or windows.

NOTES

[1] *Who Is Talking to Our Children?* ACT's Third National Symposium on Children and Television (Newtonville, MA: 1972), p. 8.

[2] *Action for Children's Television*, p. 58.

[3] F. Earle Barcus, *Television in the Afterschool Hours* (Newtonville, MA: 1975).

[4] "Children's Television: More Than Mere Entertainment," *Harvard Educational Review*, 44:2 (1974), p. 221.

[5] Rita Dohrmann "A Gender Profile of Children's Educational TV," *Journal of Communication*, 25:4 (Autumn 1975) pp. 56–65.

[6] *Who Is Talking to Our Children?* p. 58.

[7] *Who Is Talking to Our Children?* p. 30.

[8] *Who Is Talking to Our Children?* p. 18.

[9] Reprinted from December 1972 Issue of *McCall's* magazine, "You and Your Family," by Dr. Lee Salk.

[10] Rosemary Lee Potter "Making the Home-School TV Connection: Parent Conference," *Teacher* (June 1977).

[11] This pamphlet is available free from the American Optometric Association, 700 Chippewa Street, St. Louis, MO 63119.

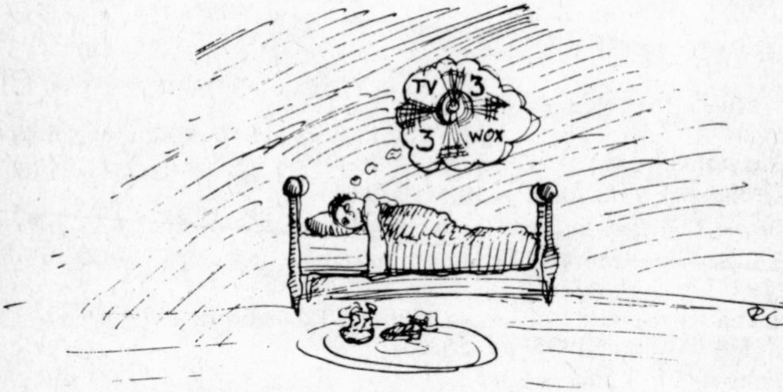

drawing by Rob Chalfen

The Business of Broadcasting

At present, American television is divided into several broadcasting outlets. The commercial broadcasters pay for programming costs by accepting commercials from advertisers. Most local commercial broadcasters are affiliated with one of the three major networks—ABC, CBS, and NBC. But any broadcaster may own up to five VHF or seven UHF stations and many of them have formed mini-networks, such as the Westinghouse, Avco, Post-Newsweek, and Meredith Broadcasting Corporations. There are also a few independent stations. (See Figure 2.)

According to data compiled by *Broadcasting Magazine,* a major industry news source, there are 996 operating television stations in the United States (see Appendix A for further broadcasting statistics). In 1975, commercial television stations had revenues of $4.1 billion, the networks accounting for over $2 billion of that total.

All broadcasting stations, both radio and television, are licensed by the Federal Communications Commission (FCC) in Washington, D.C., and must apply for license renewals every three years. (A list of major TV groups is given in the Resource Directory.)

COMMERCIAL TELEVISION

In 1971, the FCC commissioned Dr. Allan Pearce, an economist, to carry out an extensive study, *"The Economics of Children's Television Programming."* Dr. Pearce found:

In the broadcasting business, ratings determine revenue. The bigger a network's audience, the more it can charge for the time it sells to advertisers. From an advertiser's point of view, what matters is the size of the audience watching the program surrounding the commercial minutes. The ratings points, which express the numbers of television homes tuned in to a particular program, are, in effect, the only way braodcasters have yet figured out to price their merchandise, which is the time the public spends watching television.

Figure 2
BROADCASTING: HOW IT WORKS

NETWORKS

Commercial Networks:*			Non-Commercial Network:
ABC	CBS	NBC	
5 owned and operated TV stations	5 owned and operated TV stations	5 owned and operated TV stations	Owns NO stations

PROGRAM DISTRIBUTION

To 5 stations and 195 affiliates	To 5 stations and 198 affiliates	To 5 stations and 212 affiliates	Distributes to 277 non-commercial stations

FINANCIAL SUPPORT

Funds raised from advertising sales through:
  a) network commercials and sponsorship, from range of business and companies
  b) local commercials, sponsorship and promotional advertising by local companies
(In 1977, pretax profits for all three networks totaled $406 million.)

Public broadcasting funds come from:
  a) Corporation for Public Broadcasting (CPB) which administers government grants
  b) donations from viewers and major companies
  c) foundation grants
  d) annual TV auctions
  e) corporate underwriting
(Nonprofit)

PRODUCTION OF PROGRAMS

Major networks and station groups, as well as local stations, produce program series, specials and news programs or commission independent producers to make shows.

Local stations produce all programs, some of which are aired nationally.

Programs and series are purchased from independent sources or after being shown on the air, either in USA or other countries.

*There are also several major station groups such as Westinghouse and Metromedia which own up to seven TV stations. No broadcaster may own more than five VHF stations, but a broadcaster may own up to seven UHF stations. A recent FCC Policy Statement also stressed that broadcasters who own more than three stations in the top fifty markets must show special reasons why they should own more. This statement, an effort to encourage diversity of ownership, has so far had little effect.

Audience measurement ratings equate with circulation (or readership) in the print media, with one important economic difference. If a newspaper publisher has a newspaper operation that costs $1 million a day, with a daily circulation of one million and advertising revenues of $500,000 daily, he has to sell his newspapers for fifty cents each in order to break even. If a broadcaster has a product—a children's television special, for example—that costs $1 million to produce and sell at a profit, and he has an audience of a million households, it costs him one dollar for each household in the audience and he attempts to fix the rates for his commercial minutes accordingly. If the audience for the show increases to two million households, the unit cost becomes only fifty cents, and so on. The broadcaster, like the newspaper or magazine owner, can charge more for his commercial minutes because he is offering a larger audience to the advertisers, but unlike his competitors in the print media, the broadcaster's unit costs always fall once break-even point has been reached.[1]

In his excellent book, *Television: The Business Behind the Box*, Les Brown, broadcasting editor for the *New York Times*, describes what has come to be the attitude of commercial networks:

In day-to-day commerce, television is not so much interested in the business of communications as in the business of delivering people to advertisers. People are the merchandise, not the shows. The shows are merely the bait. The consumer, whom the custodians of the medium are pledged to serve, is in fact served up.[2]

Counter-Programming

The average viewer would probably prefer to be offered a choice of programs on different channels at the same time. One station could offer a movie, another a talk show, while a third aired some music or a variety hour. But we all know that movies are usually run at the same time as other movies, that talk shows run against other talk shows, and that all stations run their news programs at the same time. It is no different for children. On Saturday mornings all three commercial networks run children's programs because the majority of available viewers are children.

The pressures of ratings make it essential for a program to attract the largest share of the available audience. A network may have five million viewers for its program, but if the total available audience was twenty million and the other two networks attracted seven and a half million each, it failed.

Statistics always show that large numbers of children are watching television in the late afternoon. But the total audience contains far more adults. It is, therefore, better for the network affiliates to attract the largest share of the available audience by putting on adult programs than to lose it by putting on children's shows, even though they may attract a sizable number of children. Sometimes, when major stations are running adult shows, local independent stations will counter-program, that is, run low-cost cartoon reruns to attract the large child audience, since they feel that in the late afternoon they cannot compete in attracting the "cream" adult audience.

The only possible change in such pressures is the availability of additional television channels. As more channels become available in different areas, audiences become more specialized. Public television has already shown that quality children's TV programs, like "Sesame Street," which are well-produced and entertaining, can attract a reasonably large audience. In areas where there is no public TV, many commercial stations run "Sesame Street" without commercials because the quality of the program will attract a large number of children.

But at present, the pressures of competition are so fierce that no major station will willingly forgo its share of the audience by programming for children in the late afternoon or during the daytime on a regular basis. In the same way, the Saturday morning chase-and-bop cartoons have been shown to attract children from ages two to eleven, a wide range, while a program designed for a specific age range, say six to eleven, would lose some part of that audience and, therefore, get low ratings. Because it is essential, for maximum profits, to claim a maximum audience at all times, programming aimed at children of a specific age is likely to be quickly replaced by cartoons which can attract the broadest span of the available child audience.

PUBLIC TELEVISION

Public television is funded from sources other than advertising revenues based on ratings and has managed to provide a regular daily schedule of television programs for children of various ages. In many areas of the country, there are daytime programs designed for viewing in the schools as part of a definite curriculum. Public television is usually the only network regularly carrying such programs to the schools and cooperating with educators in this important area.

Although a few public television stations operate on VHF channels (very high frequency—channels 2 through 13), most public stations are assigned to UHF channels (ultra high frequency—channels 14 through 83). In general, UHF stations provide weaker signals and may be difficult to receive without an outside antenna. At present, a special circular antenna is needed for reasonable UHF reception.

In many areas of the country, public television stations cannot provide clear signals to all viewers because of the limitations of the UHF band. An alliance of commercial stations (led by Kaiser Broadcasting) and public broadcasting officials is urging changes in TV sets so that UHF stations can be received as clearly as VHF stations.

CABLE TELEVISION

The steady growth of cable television may transform the concept of television as we know it today. Cable TV is a way of receiving television signals through lines similar to telephone cables, instead of over the air from transmitters or satellites. Originally it was designed to improve reception in areas that were mountainous or had poor over-the-air reception. Today the industry is one of the fastest growing branches of television and recent court decisions have opened up thousands of cable TV opportunities across the country.

Cable TV increases the number of channels available so that there can be far more diversity of programming. Warner Cable, one of the nation's largest cable networks, has reserved one cable channel in its Cleveland system for children's programming, to allow parents to find suitable shows for their children at any time of day.

Educators have suggested that one channel could be used for instructional programming designed for adults, and linked to credits and degrees, as is done in some colleges now.

In areas with several stations, cable can provide services that other stations do not offer. You can find the stock market ticker tape, constant weather reports, market reports on the cost of food and other products, community news, and full-length feature films on different cable channels in New York City, for example. One apartment building puts on a weekly cable discussion program among residents which is broadcast locally. Some communities are discussing televising town council meetings or committee meetings, and there is much talk of televising court proceedings from one community to another so that policemen need not spend hours waiting to give evidence in particular cases.

A mind-boggling array of choices is possible when there are twenty-five, fifty, seventy-five, or even hundreds of channels available on a television set. However, it is the decisions that the cable operators make that will affect what we see over the next decade.

BROADCASTING AND THE INDIVIDUAL

The Communications Act of 1934 was expressly designed to stress the importance of considering the public's needs in broadcasting decisions. Stations must be operated "in the public interest, convenience and necessity," and while those three words may be interpreted in many ways, it is clear that the spirit of the act is to ensure that broadcasting is responsive to the needs of the community and the viewer.

It is most important that citizens recognize their responsibility in this area. Each individual can have a voice in expressing ideas and opinions to a local broadcaster, and groups of individuals representing major segments of a community have a clear legal right to insist that local broadcasting reflect their interests and viewpoints.

Until recently there was little awareness of the citizens' rights in broadcasting, and most broadcasters did little to inform the public of them. However, in recent years pressure from groups concerned about the lack of representation of various ideas and philosophies has begun to bring about some changes. In the sensitive area of broadcasting for children, it is even more vital that issues such as racism, sexism, and discrimination be carefully examined, and that broadcasters be always aware that programs must meet the needs of the wide variety of children in the viewing audience.

NOTES

[1] *The Economics of Children's Television Programming* (Washington, D.C.: 1972), pp. 3–4.
[2] *Television: The Business Behind the Box* (New York: 1971), p. 15.

Children's TV Programming

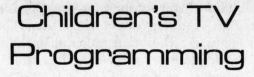

The growth of television in the 1950s and '60s prompted a change in American weekend living patterns. Saturday morning became "prime time" for network children's programming. While adults were busy with household chores, children were mesmerized by cartoons, cartoons, and more cartoons. The quality of network children's offerings ranged from the inane to the innocuous. The monster cartoons of the late '60s have given way to some live action dramas and cartoons with strong "prosocial" messages, but throughout the history of network children's television, the broadcasters' primary concern has been meeting the needs of the advertisers rather than the needs of children and their parents.

One technique which networks have used to assuage mounting parental criticism without changing the substance of regular Saturday morning fare is to introduce short educational segments between regular programs. CBS has initiated "In the News," a well-produced series of two-and-a-half-minute features which presents items from the week's news simply and informatively. ABC's "Schoolhouse Rock," a series of three-minute musical interpretations of math, grammar, and history concepts, is both entertaining and educational. And in 1977, NBC introduced ninety-second biographies of youngsters with special skills and interests into its Saturday morning schedule. Entitled "Junior Hall of Fame," NBC hopes that the series will "make the kids feel they're not powerless in the world in which they live . . . (and) make kids aware of other opportunities they may want to avail themselves of."

Yet the bulk of Saturday morning programs show little regard for children's interests or vulnerabilities. Thoughtful programming remains the exception rather than the rule, and, all too often, conscientious programming efforts are the first to be cancelled in broadcasting's ratings scramble. NBC, whose Saturday morning schedule continually trails the line-ups of ABC and CBS, recently abandoned the best of its programs to revive outdated cartoon series such as "Hong Kong Phooey." And Saturday morning's much-touted "umbrella format," in which short program segments are tied together by animated or musical wrap-arounds, has proved to be just another device to prevent children from changing channels in the middle of their morning viewing.

CHILDREN'S HOUR CHOICES

Looking through the TV listings you may despair of finding a "balanced diet" of programs for your children to watch in the afternoon or early evening hours. Public television is the only network airing regular daily shows for children during the late afternoon hours. However, many communities do not receive public television, and others find it difficult to receive because it is on a UHF station and may not give a clear picture on the screen.

Early evening is recognized in most Western countries as the time when adults are busy preparing for the evening meal, tired from the work day and coping with children who are also tired and perhaps hungry as well. American commercial broadcasters recognize this audience by airing old series interspersed with the usual assault of ads directed mainly at children.

The choice is often between reruns of old movies, game shows, old adult series, or even older cartoons, which often had been dropped by the networks because of protests before they were put into syndication.

Most of the programs on the air in the late afternoon were originally produced for an adult audience. They were first aired in the evening as adult shows. Now, according to the reasoning of TV station program managers, the passage of time has made them suitable for children.

Let us look at a case history. "Bewitched" began some years ago with the usual new-season ballyhoo as an evening series; it was about a woman living in the twentieth century, attractive, personable, and modern, who happened to be a witch. The series was based on the humorous, unusual, and unlikely situations in which she found herself when she used her witchcraft to solve problems. In 1972 the series was aired by ABC at 11:00 A.M. as a children's Saturday morning program. It is also in syndication and has been broadcast in the late afternoon, when there is a large child audience. Further, an animated cartoon series based on "Bewitched," "Sabrina, the Teenage Witch," was run by CBS on its Saturday morning children's schedule.

There are other adult series which follow the same pattern. Some have humor, some adventure, some violence. The essential point for parents to remember is that none of these series was designed with children in mind. The programs were all planned for an adult audience, to appeal to mass tastes, and to be shown in the evening hours.

Afternoon commercial television does offer occasional highlights, and ABC's "Afterschool Specials" may exemplify the best of children's television drama. Now in their fifth season, the specials have examined a wide range of issues including alcoholism ("Francesca, Baby"); divorce ("Me and Dad's New Wife"); childbirth ("My Mom's Having a Baby"); and the death of a sibling ("Very Good Friends") with sensitivity and good taste.

NBC's "Special Treat" is the afterschool counterpart of the ABC specials and has presented a variety of outstanding children's programming in its first two years. The series has featured dramatizations of children's novels such as "Big Henry and the Polka Dot Kid" and documentaries on topics such as television stuntmen and the Beatles. NBC has also organized parent participation workshops, where parents and children can meet to discuss their reactions to the programs.

CBS broadcasts its "Festival of the Lively Arts for Young People," bringing music, dance, and opera to youngsters, about six times each year.

The networks' commitment to at least one quality afterschool series demonstrates their ability to produce exceptional programming when they set their minds to it. One independent producer who has produced shows for all three networks in afterschool hours comments that each one takes a different approach to children's specials: "ABC is interested in telling a story which embodies a lesson in living or a sort of moral; CBS is getting into more classical areas like opera, ballet or theater but providing the shows with a popular motif; NBC seems to be more involved with shows that are educationally oriented."

The costs of producing such shows is high. ABC pays $175,000 for a sixty-minute children's special for which it gets two runs at present.

Some local stations have responded to increased demand for quality children's series by creating innovative new programs. Westinghouse Broadcasting's (Group W) "Call It Macaroni" brings new activities to the attention of seven- to twelve-year-olds by profiling youngsters involved in such diverse recreations as visiting the Cloisters in New York, attending dance classes with Alvin Ailey, learning to play bluegrass in Nashville, and meeting an Eskimo family in Alaska.

"Kidsworld," a delightful and entertaining children's magazine, is produced by Behrens Company, a syndicator, and is distributed to local stations across the country. Hosted by children aged eight to twelve, the program includes news clips gathered from local stations that broadcast the show.

And surprisingly, more than fifty commercial TV stations run "Sesame Street" without commercials in areas where there is no public television.

These changes and improvements in children's television have occurred partly because of outside pressure, as network executives freely admit.

Squire Rushnell, vice-president of Children's and Early Morning Programing at ABC-TV, gives credit to Action for Children's Television. "The group gave an important impetus to change the industry's attitude toward children's TV," he said recently in New York. "ACT has been one of the most effective grass roots organizations in America. If ACT went away tomorrow, it would be to the detriment of me and my colleagues and of those within the industry who have been working to change children's TV."[1]

George Heinemann, children's specialist at NBC, was the creator of "Ding Dong School," one of the first network children's series. He has commented: "ACT wanted more variety and diversity of programs, shows on in the late afternoon and not just Saturday mornings, more live action and less animation, a lessening of violence, and more concern for the messages and the quality of programs. These major changes are continuing because people have learned that there is not a schism between education and entertainment in the broadcast sense."[2]

However, all these changes mean that parents must know when new programs are broadcast. Only then can they encourage their children to watch and enjoy the best of what broadcasters have put together.

HOW CHILDREN'S PROGRAMS ARE MADE

Until 1970, no network and few local commercial stations had any qualified individuals responsible for children's programs. The daytime program producer took charge of the few children's shows that were scattered among the quiz shows, soap operas, and games. In January 1970, ACT representatives met in New York with several CBS officials, and discussed with them the issue of responsibility for children's programs, among other things. This meeting was reported in the *New York Times* and shortly afterward all three commercial TV networks appointed vice-presidents for children's programming. A few local stations also appointed special producers for children's programs. However, since the new appointments were not accompanied by adequate funding or commitment of facilities for producing and planning children's programs, the vice-presidents became public relations figureheads for network efforts to upgrade programming. Even now, there is no permanent children's television unit in any commercial network and no long-term planning for children's programming over the next few years.

In order to develop a creative, constructive TV series, time is needed for research and preparation, and there must be a commitment of creativity and originality as well as a clear awareness that the measure of the program's success is its ability to meet the needs of children. In network television, the pressures to attract high ratings make it undesirable for producers to design experimental programs on a wide variety of subjects. Instead, most network executives have decided that children's programs must be animated cartoons.

A brief summary of the different production methods in three different kinds of children's series will provide some idea of how such decisions are made.

Network Animated Cartoons

On Saturday mornings, networks air their children's programs. Most of the series are produced in the Los Angeles area by large animation companies such as Hanna-Barbera, and use the same artists, voices, and music. Consequently, there is a great similarity among the programs.

Many cartoons on television now use a form of limited animation, where only the eyes and mouths of the characters move. This is much less expensive and quicker to produce than the full animation used in older cartoons. Music, dialogue, and sound effects are plugged in last rather than carefully synchronized. Worst of all is the added artificial laugh track, which can hardly modify the violence, explosions, and confusion in these cartoons. The chief concern of the animation companies seems to be to turn out their product in the cheapest and easiest way. All the network asks of the animators is that they provide the required amount of cartoon material for airing at the right time with the right holes for commercials; the network's main concern is to attract advertising in order to make its profits. And all the animator asks of the network is to be paid.

Local broadcasters decide whether to air a network program, or whether to replace it with a local program. They can also insert local commercials. According to the broadcasting regulations, it is the local broadcaster who is responsible for what is aired on the stations. Broadcasters should be aware of the programs they show. But few broadcasters preview or even watch the networks' animated cartoons.

Decisions about children's program series are made by network executives in the spring. Since it is generally accepted at network level that animated cartoons attract the largest audience of children aged two to eleven, there has been little change in the format for the Saturday morning lineup for several years. Network executives do not plan a varied five-hour span of programming for children from 8:00 A.M. to 1:00 P.M., but simply invite animation companies to submit ideas to fill that time with cartoons. These ideas, in the form of story outlines or drawings on story boards, are presented to the executives, who then decide what to order. Usually a series runs thirteen or twenty-six weeks with an agreement about the number of reruns and airings. There is little discussion about the value of such programs or the lack of diversity that results from the three networks scheduling fifteen hours of animated cartoons on Saturday morning. There is little examination of the implications of the story lines, the characters, or the settings in terms of their impact on children. Little testing or research of any kind is done on program segments or pilots with groups of children or parents. The networks have few standards or guidelines for the programming, and the animation companies certainly don't expect to be involved in research or content examination at any point.

Noncommercial Programs

Most noncommercial programs for children have been designed in a totally different way even though they too use a certain amount of animation and cartoon formats. "Sesame Street," a one-hour daily program designed to teach preschool children the alphabet and numbers, uses animation in its letter and number segments. "The Electric Company," a half-hour daily program teaching older children how to read, uses animation and computer-designed graphics to illustrate phonics, letter combinations, and specific words. Both series are produced by the Children's Television Workshop in New York City, a nonprofit corporation.

Prior to production a great deal of time was spent discussing the goals and aims of both of these series. Many meetings and conferences were held with child development experts, parents, researchers, teachers, and others to examine what was essential and what should be omitted in the programs. Almost a year was spent in research and preparation before the first program of "Sesame Street" went on the air. This meant that the Children's Television Workshop had to spend part of its grant to support itself and its staff while the preparation of the program was taking place. But it recognized that this was vital to the success of the program and repeated the process with "The Electric Company."

After the basic content was decided upon, the elements of the material were broken into segments and given to writers, designers, animators, and graphic artists. Each tried to devise the best way to present the educational idea successfully on television. The work of the producer was to segment the work; the work of the director was to translate the creative work of the individual segments into a cohesive whole. Since both "Sesame Street" and "The Electric Company" are videotaped, much of the programs' appeal lies in judicious and accurate editing of the segments into programs.

In contrast to network attitudes toward their animated cartoons, the Children's Television Workshop is actively interested in every portion of its programs before they go on the air. Segments are carefully screened, examined, and viewed by experts and by children to see if the educational aims are achieved. When a program is being aired in schools, researchers check reactions, teachers' opinions, and children's comments. The Children's Television Workshop has a special viewing room set up for showing children sections and whole programs in order to study the effects of the series on a particular audience.

The Children's Television Workshop has carried out several major studies to judge the teaching effectiveness of the program, and to find out what children have learned from the series, especially those from inner-city or low-income areas. In recent years, non-English-speaking characters have been integrated into the "Sesame Street" cast and there has been an increased use of Spanish within the series.

Participatory Television   One of the few television series that encourages active participation by children is "ZOOM!," a weekly half-hour program produced by WGBH-TV, Boston, and aired nationally on public television.

"ZOOM!" is designed to appeal to children aged six to twelve, and all the material on the program is sent in by the audience. The stories, plays, jokes, riddles, games, and tongue-twisters submitted are performed on the program by a group of seven children, chosen as representative of the audience. The cast changes every twenty-six weeks, in order to give as broad a range of children as possible a chance to appear on the show. The program also includes filmed segments of children doing interesting things in other parts of the country: a girl rodeo rider, a boy baking bread, two boys who catch fish and bake them in mud, a twelve-year-old fiddler from Appalachia, and a blind boy who designed a wooden spintop game.

In January 1974 over 25,000 letters a week were flooding into the stations with suggestions and material for the series. Initially sorted by volunteers, the poems, plays, jokes, and ideas

are then sent to the program's staff and cast. They jointly agree on what they like and think will work, and then plan the details of rehearsing plays, reading jokes, and the other aspects of the show. The seven cast members contribute their own ideas and make suggestions about ways of presenting other children's material. Presentations of games and discussions in the studio are unscripted and videotaped live.

Only at the final stage of fitting the material into a half-hour show, with the technical details of editing film and tape, timing segments, and adding music, is there a total adult involvement. Otherwise, the program is wholly created and produced by children, their ideas and contributions.

The viewing audience's criticisms and comments are carefully read by the program staff, and are often adopted in future programs. "ZOOM!" is particularly concerned with the needs of its audience and has an unusual and immediate gauge for measuring the show's effectiveness in this mail response: 10,000 letters a week still arrive for the show.

Commercial Programs

Children's Drama: ABC Afterschool Specials Since the beginning of this series three years ago, Daniel Wilson Productions has produced ten of the one-hour dramas for children aired in the afternoon. Every show has been exceptional in its choice of topic, professional production, and quality of presentation, and several of the programs have won awards.

Each show, budgeted at around $200,000, begins with a carefully chosen theme—for instance, stories about adopted children and children's rights might be considered. If there are no published books or materials on a suggested theme, a writer is asked to produce either a treatment (outline) or a script. When the final script is approved by ABC, production begins in California. A production team is put together, and actors cast in the parts. The drama is always filmed on location, not in a studio. There is no advisory board nor is there an examination of the impact of the program, though extensive research into the topic is conducted before the drama is written.

"We are really trying to do important themes in a dramatic

form, and the most important thing is that it be well written," explained Wilson from his New York office.

Production usually takes between six and nine months. Programs are aired on ABC and then distributed as films through Time-Life, Inc. Many schools and libraries make use of the films.

Big Blue Marble   The first world-wide children's television series, "Big Blue Marble," is presented as a public service without commercials by International Telephone and Telegraph Corporation (ITT), which pays for all production and syndication costs. The series, broadcast on local stations across the country, has already won Emmy and Peabody awards for children's television programming.

The programs are made up of seven- to ten-minute segments about the lives of children in other countries, filmed on location by experienced film-makers and then edited into a half-hour magazine format. There are short pieces on crafts, music, food, and animated folktales; there is a special pen pal invitation to encourage children around the world to write to each other. The name of the program comes from a comment made by one of the astronauts as he flew to the moon. From space, he noted, the Earth was like "a big blue marble."

The series began in 1975 and is now broadcast in more than sixty countries.

CHILDREN WITH SPECIAL NEEDS

Coinciding with the opening day of the White House Conference on Handicapped Individuals in Washington, D.C., Action for Children's Television brought out a first-of-its-kind resource collection about television and children with special needs.[3] Entitled *Promise and Performance: ACT's Guide to TV Programming for Children, Volume I: Children with Special Needs*, the book is edited by Maureen Harmonay, with a foreword by Julius B. Richmond, M.D., who was recently appointed surgeon general of the U.S.

The collection contains twenty-five original articles by broadcasters, educators, psychologists, and researchers, who discuss the images of disabled people in the media; the effect of television programming on the mental health and self-concepts of children; the needs of children in hospitals; TV programs about parenting; and past TV productions that have included children with handicaps.

Among the contributing writers are representatives from the nationally syndicated series "Big Blue Marble," "Call It Macaroni," "Mister Rogers' Neighborhood," "Sesame Street," and "Zoom!" These broadcasting professionals provide unprecedented first-hand analyses of their diverse experiences in scripting, filming, and producing adventure documentaries, cameo portraits, and dramatic and educational programs about children with a variety of special needs.

Promise and Performance, Volume I, is the first in a series of resource books about the ways in which producers of children's programs can enhance, enrich, and engage the young members of their audience. The series will include books on programming about the arts, sciences, consumer education, and role models for young adolescents.

WHAT HAPPENS IN OTHER COUNTRIES?

An unpublished National Citizens Committee for Broadcasting survey of children's TV in sixteen countries (Austria, Australia, Canada, Denmark, Finland, France, Britain, Ireland, Italy, Japan, the Netherlands, Norway, Sweden, Switzerland, the United States, and West Germany) found that in 1971 the United States was the only major country where television networks did not carry weekday afternoon programs for children. The other findings of the study were:

— America allows more advertising on children's programs than any other country surveyed.
— Only four nations allow advertising on children's programs on some channels: the United States, England, Japan and Canada.
— While American programs often span a two- to twelve-year-old range, children's TV in other countries tends to be designated for more specific age groups.

Television in many countries is very different from television in the United States. Some have only one or two channels which do not operate all day long. In those where advertising is allowed, it is strictly controlled in length and time when it can be aired. The intensive pressures of ratings and competitive programming are almost unknown outside of the United States. But as other countries expand their hours of broadcasting and the number of channels, and begin to depend more on commercial support, they may have to face the same problems America does today.

Canada

It is worth noting that just to the north, Canada is providing an interesting range of programs for children on a regular basis. Many Canadian parents have joined ACT or formed local organizations concerned with children's TV because they are critical of programs and advertising beamed across the border from the United States.

Canadian TV stations, both public and private, ceased advertising to preschool children in January 1974, and have adopted a voluntary code of restraint in advertising to children generally.

In addition, there is no advertising during children's programs on the government-supported Canadian Broadcasting Corporation (CBC) network or stations, or on any publicly-owned radio or television station; this is one of the conditions for license renewal. This ban came into effect in January 1975, in response to a report of the Canadian Radio-Television Commission (the Canadian equivalent of the FCC).

Children's television in Canada comes from several production centers. French-language programs are produced in Montreal by Radio-Canada (the French service of the CBC), and include "Nik et Pik," a series of the delightful adventures of two puppet mice traveling around the world; "Sol et Gobelet," a series about two clowns; "Bobino," a daily program now in its eighteenth season; and "Franfrelouche," a series linked by a puppet-doll who gets involved with familiar fairy stories and changes them around.

In Toronto, CBC provides nineteen hours of children's TV

each week, including "Mr. Dress Up" and "Friendly Giant" for preschool children and "The Fit-Stop," an exercise and health program, for older children. CBC also produces special segments about children and situations in various parts of Canada which are inserted into "Sesame Street" programs to give them a more Canadian outlook.

Australia

According to data compiled by John P. Murray for an international survey of children's television published in *Phaedrus*[4] in the spring of 1978, recent studies show that Australian children watch about three hours of TV every day. Younger children watch less than older children.

Children's programs range from cartoons to general children's entertainment/information programs, and include in-school instructional programs. In 1975–76 public stations broadcast about 80 hours of cartoons, 970 hours of children's general/preschool programs, and 640 hours of educational programs. Commercial television aired 370 hours of cartoons, 350 hours of general/preschool programs, and no formal educational programs.

Children's programs for public stations are produced primarily by the Australian Broadcasting Company. Various private production houses supply commercial stations.

Like the United States, cartoons and reruns of shows like "The Lucy Show," "I Dream of Jeannie," and "My Three Sons" are broadcast during the late afternoon. A children's program committee has been proposed which would be responsible for reviewing and classifying all programs for commercial television that are suitable for viewing by children aged six to twelve.

Advertising regulations stipulate that commercial stations may not exceed eleven minutes per hour from 7:00 P.M. to 10:00 P.M. and thirteen minutes per hour at other times during weekdays and Saturdays. On Sunday, advertising may not exceed six minutes per hour from 6:00 A.M. to 12:00 noon and nine minutes per hour for the rest of the day.

Performers and hosts on children's programs are prohibited

from endorsing advertised products in the context of the program, and a recent report proposed the elimination of advertising in preschool programs. The report also suggested that "prosocial" messages relating to health, safety, and nutrition may be included during children's programming time blocks.

England

In England, the British Broadcasting Corporation (BBC) funded by fees collected from the public and government grants, airs children's programs without commercials. Commercial television permits six minutes of ads per hour at "natural breaks." This means ads are usually confined to the hour, half-hour, or quarter-hour breaks, but rarely interrupt the flow of a program. There are the same number of ads on children's programs as on adult shows.

The March 1977 Annan Commission Report on the Future of Broadcasting examined the issue of advertising in children's programming and proposed: "There should be no advertisements within children's programs or between two programs designed for children." Moreover, the report suggested that "advertisements promoting products or services of particular interest to children should not be shown before 9:00 P.M."

In discussing the topic, the report notes that removing advertising would mean a loss of 15 million pounds (about $30 million) annually, but concluded: "The majority of us believe that children should not be exposed during their own programs to the blandishments and subtle persuasiveness of advertising."

The report will be examined and discussed in 1978 before its proposals are acted upon.

It should also be noted that England has only three television channels, and that the number of programs aired by them is far smaller than that shown by Amerian television.

It is only in the United States that such an enormous quantity of television is constantly available, that programs are transmitted twenty-four hours a day, seven days a week. This means that parents and children involved in decisions about television viewing have to recognize that such decisions affect almost their every waking moment. In many other countries, the quantity of television available is so limited that the decisions are only necessary once or twice a day. In Sweden, for example, there is no commercial television at all and all children's programming is noncommercial, on two channels, for a couple of hours daily.

Prix Jeunesse

The *Prix Jeunesse* (Youth Prize) is an international television award given to outstanding television productions for children and young people. The *Prix Jeunesse* Foundation was established in 1964 by the Free State of Bavaria, the city of Munich, and the Bavarian Broadcasting Corporation, to promote programs for the young and to award prizes for the best productions. It aims to both foster competition and be a forum for communication, exchange of information, and improvement of production standards. A conference is held every two years in Munich, Germany, under the auspices of the European Broadcasting Union and UNESCO. The participants select the prize-winning programs. Most of the participants are European, Canadian, Japanese, or Australian, although many countries with limited television resources also attend. Very few Americans ever participate or submit programs; the conference is given little publicity in the United States.

Although American programs are rarely shown at *Prix Jeunesse* meetings, there have been some exceptions in the last two or three years: several noncommercial children's programs— "ZOOM!," "Sesame Street," "The Electric Company," "Carroscelendas"—have been shown and were well received.

ACT ACHIEVEMENT AWARDS

When ACT began in 1968, the standard of children's programs was so low that clearly poor programming and overcommercialization were the major issues.

Now, a decade later, the picture has changed. There are still problems with children's television, but there is at least variety and diversity in some areas of programming. Some of the people working in television have begun to understand that children are an important and sensitive audience that needs special attention and that they deserve programs designed for their age level and understanding.

In response to these changes, ACT created its Achievement Awards to recognize and compliment achievement and creativity within the field of children's television. The awards are given to producers and performers, underwriting companies, and network representatives who have shown concern and awareness for the needs of young audiences. In the past few years there have been many outstanding programs that have received awards and a complete list of these programs is provided in Appendix C.

NOTES

[1] From an interview in "Children's TV: What Really Happened," *Videography* magazine, June 1977.
[2] Ibid.
[3] Cambridge, MA: 1977.
[4] An international journal of children's research, published in Marblehead, MA.

How to Treat TV with T.L.C.*
*Tender Loving Care

Children learn from everything they watch on television. They learn from the earnest science program that attempts to explain gravity directly, and they learn from the news program that depicts the ways in which men can live in space. They learn from variety shows and comedy hours. They learn from public television's educational series and from commercial television's adventure series. They learn from snappy commercials and well-meaning public service announcements. And they learn very quickly how to turn on the TV set and where the stations are on the dial. "Sesame Street" researchers found that preschool children had little trouble tuning the set to the station airing the program—even though it might be a high-numbered UHF channel.

It is impossible to separate "entertainment" from "education" for children under twelve when they're watching TV. How can the dramatic television series "Roots" be classified as entertainment when the educational implications of the programs were direct and impressive? Or how can a musical sequence on "Captain Kangaroo" be considered mere entertainment if it leads a child to try writing a song or picking out the tunes on the piano?

Moreover, even if all shows children watch were delightful and sensitive, the deluge of television programs in the United States makes it imperative to make some choices. Children who watch thirty or forty hours a week of television, even at its best, are missing out on some important learning opportunities: playing with friends, reading books, drawing pictures, even daydreaming.

So what can responsible parents do? Can we teach our children to make selective choices about what to watch? And what are the criteria?

CRITERIA

The setting of standards is always a difficult task. Personal taste is the ultimate factor in any decision, and it is hard to establish rules that take individual opinions into account. Many teenagers love the humor of the British "Monty Python" series aired on public TV stations, but adults are divided about the program's suitability for young viewers. Some feel the series is vulgar, while others praise its humor as zany and unique. Opinions often differ about a child's ability to understand TV messages.

One station ran a series of spots warning children about the dangers of drug use, with a major TV star as the host. There were two reactions: one group of parents felt the spots were helpful; another group felt that they taught children that although drugs were naughty, trying them might be fun.

The following are suggestions for questions you might want to ask about the programs you and your children see.

General Criteria
1. *For Whom Is The Program Designed?*

- young children
- children from six to eleven
- teenagers
- adults only
- all ages

The program *fails* if it is too complicated for young children;

- if it is too simplistic for older children;
- if it is too diffuse in its approach so that no one likes it;
- if it is totally unsuitable for its audience, because of subject matter, approach, treatment.

2. How Much Violence Is There?

- The program *succeeds* if the violence is an integral part of the plot and essential to its development, but not excessive.
- The program *fails* if there is an excessive amount of violence used merely to add excitement and to attract the attention of child viewers.

3. How Appropriate Is a Situation Comedy?

- The program *succeeds* if the characters are multi-dimensional and develop over the length of the series;
    - if the characters form meaningful relationships within the humorous context of the program;
    - if the series occasionally incorporates important social messages;
    - if the program avoids directing humor at one particular segment of society.

- The program fails if the humor consistently insults one particular group.
    - if the situations are cruel, unpleasant or sadistic;
    - if the children misinterpret the program's humor in ways that you find disturbing;
    - if an excessively loud laugh track is used to punctuate every line.

4. How Scary Is Scary?

- The program *succeeds* if the episodes and incidents are an integral part of the plot, but not terrifying or upsetting to child viewers.
- The program *fails* if the scariness is added only to give excitement to a story of poor quality;
    - if incidents are frightening beyond the limits acceptable for the age range of its audience.

5. How Are the Characters Portrayed?

The presentation and portrayal of characters on TV is a sensitive and important issue. Statistics show that white males predominate on both adult and children's programs, and that the "bad guys" are often dark, foreign, and non-English-speaking.

When you watch a children's program, try to decide whether the characters are realistically portrayed or whether they are stereotypes.

- The program *succeeds* if the characters are convincing;
  - if the characters within a program demonstrate a diversity of backgrounds, views, and interests.

- The program *fails* if the casting of characters consistently shows stereotyped thinking, i.e., bad guys dark, good guys blond, women foolish;
  - if your child imitates the characters in a manner that you find disturbing.

6. What About the Plot?

Once the characters in a series have been established, story lines are developed. Dialogue is then filled out by script writers. The choice of topics for the story lines may depend on the producer, the executive producer, the director, the writer, or in some cases the actors in the cast.

In evaluating a program's suitability for young viewers, it is important to remember that a child's understanding of a television story may differ from an adult's. Researchers have found that many children cannot accurately repeat a television story line until age seven or eight. Social lessons or implications that are perfectly clear to older children may become mixed moral messages for younger viewers. Some important questions to ask about your child's viewing include:

- Can your child differentiate television fiction from television fact?

- Does your child understand the plot's development?

- Are the moral values implied in the story acceptable to you?

- Does the plot falsify historic events beyond an acceptable point of dramatic license?
- Do you consider such falsification misleading and/or dangerous?

7. What Happens After the Program?

Many experts are concerned about children's reactions to television. Several studies (see bibliography) show that children may act out incidents, may show more aggression or cooperation after certain types of programs, and may pursue suggestions implied in programs.

- The program *succeeds* if the child recognizes what the program has been about and can talk about it if desired;
  - if the child wants to pursue constructive follow-up activities related to the program.
- The program *fails* if the child is confused about what the program meant and is disturbed by some of its incidents or events.

8. What About Interruptions?

Commercials, public service announcements, and promotions for other programs, together with the usual barrage of station identifications, can mean confusing interruptions.

Broadcasters are responsible for what goes on the air between children's programs just as they are responsible for the programs themselves. Look carefully for:

- Commercials promoting products unhealthy or hazardous to children.
- Commercials that exploit a child's trust.
- Commercials that mislead, exaggerate, or overstate a product's attributes.
- Public service announcements that are not directed at children.
- Promos for adult programs showing disturbing scenes.
- Promos and commercials for adult films.
- News announcements that can confuse or upset children.

The major difference between television and other media experiences is TV's constant presence. If you take your child to a movie or live theater, you can carefully choose the performance, the topic, and the time when you want to go. It will be a once-only event, and you can deal with any questions prompted by the experience immediately. On the other hand, the sheer quantity of television programming makes it virtually impossible for an adult to supervise every moment of a child's viewing, especially when the child is of school age. Unless you spend every moment with your children when they are watching TV, you will have to make some general rules about viewing. And even if you did sit by your child all the time, you could not predict what exactly will be shown, or what kinds of promotion for adult shows, commercials, or public service announcements will interrupt the program.

In view of the cumulative effect of TV watching, we should adopt the same approach to television that we have to our schools. We are concerned that the schools to which we send our children follow a general trend of education and methods acceptable to us. We don't expect one particular class to teach everything, nor do we expect every teacher to be perfect. But we hope that the cumulative effect of the days our children spend in school will encourage them to learn and to appreciate knowledge for its own sake.

Since we know that children spend more time with television than they do in school, we have every right to expect and demand that the TV programs designed for our children aim for the highest ideals and do so as creatively and attractively as possible.

RANGE OF PROGRAMS

Ideally, to meet the needs of the different aspects of the child audience, broadcasters should present as broad a range of programs as they possibly can. Children should be able to watch dramas, documentaries, adventure films, comedy series, and cartoons, and decide from these experiences what they like. It is essential that alternatives be offered, no matter how high or low the ratings.

Unfortunately, commercial television today is concerned mainly with rating figures and audience-share statistics, so that networks want programs that will attract the largest portion of the available audience at any one time. Since animated cartoons can be watched by two-year-olds, five-year-olds, seven-year-olds, as well as older children, most of the programs on commercial television are animated cartoons. Fairy stories are animated, adult drama is animated, comedy series are animated. On Saturday morning network shows, often the only live people are in the commercials.

While there is nothing sinful about animation, it is sad to think that our children are watching nothing else. Television's dramatic and powerful effect is its ability to transport us to different places, to be a window to the world. If children see nothing but pint-sized animated figures on the screen, they have no chance to experience the wide range of programming that could be available to them. They have no exposure to a story acted by human beings, to films from other parts of the world, or to unusual and experimental uses of television. Their horizon is limited to stock story lines, stereotyped animation, and a repetitive format. They are being deprived of artistic alternatives.

"... No, he can't really fly ... no, the bad guys don't really have a ray gun ... no, this cereal really isn't the best food in the whole world ... no, it won't make you as strong as a giant ..."

© 1978, Sidney Harris.

WHAT PARENTS CAN DO

Parents, of course, are responsible for what their children watch on TV. Yet very little has been done by those working within the world of TV to help parents with that enormous responsibility. Parents need up-to-date information about the children's programming that is offered, as well as information about the adult programs in the afternoon and early evening that their children are likely to see. There are parents who feel that some adult evening programs are of higher caliber than afternoon shows and prefer to have their children watch those. Others feel that youngsters cannot comprehend adult evening series and limit viewing to children's programs.

As we've said before, try to spend some time watching the programs your child wants to see and find out how you feel about them. If you feel strongly that your child should not be watching them, make some appropriate rules. If you feel that "they're not doing any harm," at least you'll have some knowledge about the images and stories your child is seeing.

You Are Not Alone

Over the past few years more and more parents have come to recognize the necessity for making some rules about TV viewing. A recent poll by the Roper Organization showed that 49 percent of the families surveyed imposed strict watching rules on children six and younger; 69 percent had rules for seven- to twelve-year-olds, and 37 percent had rules for children from thirteen to sixteen.

The rules will differ depending on the age and the temperament of the child. Some workable rules might be:

For Under Sixes

Keep the TV set in a place where you will know when it's on and what children are watching. Preschool children need immediate explanations and comfort if something unexpected occurs and you should be aware of what it is.

Have time limits that your child will recognize, and perhaps invent follow-up activities related to the programs. If Captain

Kangaroo sang a particular song, perhaps you can find a record with similar songs, or draw a picture of the characters in the song, or play a game related to the activities in it. Children's Television Workshop has published materials suggesting follow-up activities for young children who watch "Sesame Street" and "Electric Company" which many parents and other adults find helpful.

Recognize that your child reacts differently when he or she is tired, hungry, sick, or restless. Some children react differently when they are watching with friends, and others like to talk about what's on the screen.

Encourage your children to tell you what they think about what's on television, and make sure that there's no confusion. Short news bulletins of sudden importance—a plane hijacking, a presidential statement—suddenly inserted in the middle of a cartoon program can easily frighten a young child. If a parent or responsible adult is there, an on-the-spot explanation can provide security and comfort immediately.

Children Between Six and Twelve

Children at this stage can usually understand the need for some rules about TV, especially if you take the time to talk about television and discuss acceptable limitations. You might begin by suggesting: "I think TV is taking too much time out of our lives, and I'd like to set some times when the TV is off and not used at all." There may be some strong reactions at first, but if you stick to your point and are determined to see that the set is not kept on as background all day, rules can be established and enforced.

Children during these years begin to watch adult shows like "Good Times" and "M*A*S*H*," and it's important that you know what they are looking at. Try to sit through a couple of episodes of the series they watch so that you'll have some idea of what's going on. All police series are not alike, nor are all comedy or variety shows. Some shows may discuss controversial topics like rape, women's liberation, divorce, homosexuality in ways that you find distasteful. This is a golden opportunity to find out how your child feels about such topics and to—gently—

voice your own opinion and express your views. Children respect your stand on topics like integration, freedom of speech, and drug use. If television is the catalyst for bringing up such topics, take advantage of the opportunity to let your child know how you feel.

Your comments will be listened to, if expressed fairly, because researchers have found that when viewing with others, children are much influenced by the reactions of those with them. "The Electric Company In-School Utilization Study: The 1971–72 School and Teacher Surveys" was carried out for Children's Television Workshop by the Center for the Study of Education, Institute for Social Research, of Florida State University, in conjunction with the Statistics Research Division of the Research Triangle Institute. Findings revealed that involvement in the series was encouraged by discussion before, during, or after viewing. More than 60 percent of the teachers said that discussion *during* the viewing time was helpful. Over 90 percent considered it helpful to hold discussions about the program immediately afterward.

Children Over Thirteen

Teenagers usually know what they want to watch and feel they are old enough to make their own decisions. If there's a particular program you don't want your teenager to see, express your views firmly, and offer an alternative program or activity in its place. Be prepared for a discussion and state your reasons clearly. Teenagers generally find rules that allow them a set number of hours of watching time each week more acceptable than limited program selection.

Special Times

In every household there are times when the best-laid plans fall apart. You may find that sickness, unexpected crises at work, visitors, or an emergency can undermine the rules you have so carefully established. Don't panic—wait until the crisis period is over, and then say something like: "Well, it's been difficult around here lately, but let's go back to those rules about TV we had before." It may mean some renegotiating, but it's always easier to set limits the second time around when you're working with an accepted idea.

QUESTIONS PARENTS ASK

Question: What's wrong with children watching cartoons?

Answer: It depends on the cartoon. If parents feel that a cartoon depicts a well-told story with animation that enhances the story, then it is probably a good program. The criteria for a good program are similar, no matter what the program format. "Sesame Street" and "Electric Company" use animation in many segments. So does an extremely violent Japanese-made cartoon about car-racing adventures called "Speed Racer." But the two programs are totally different. In much the same way as a story can be published as a paperback, a hard-cover book, a series of magazine articles, or a one-page synopsis, so can a children's story idea be translated into a variety of formats. The integrity of the interpretation, the quality of the production, and your personal taste are the only criteria that you can consistently trust.

Question: What about children watching soap operas? They're on in the afternoon when many children are home.

Answer: There are some people who find that children are bored by the talkiness of soap operas. Others are much more concerned that children not watch real people suffer in an excessively dramatic fashion when they don't understand what's happening. Other parents feel that soap operas are like other adult programs and probably should not be watched by children on a regular basis. Our experience has been that the general content of most soap operas is not really designed to meet the needs of young children and that the style of presentation can often confuse and disturb them. Certainly soap operas are not considered children's programs by broadcasters, even though they are aired during daytime hours.

Question: If the programs are so bad, why don't parents just get rid of the television set?

Answer: Some parents do take that solution. On the other hand, television is so much a part of our environment today that a child will probably see it at a friend's home, at school, or in many other situations even if there is no set at home. We, as parents, have to give our children some kind of example about living with television. It is most difficult for us because our grandparents and parents didn't have to cope with this problem to any degree. Children learn that there are rules about crossing the street, about brushing teeth, about not eating dangerous substances; in the same way they can learn that television is only one aspect of their lives and should not overwhelm all other activities.

Question: We are careful about what our young children see on TV, but during children's programs on commercial television there are often ads for adult movies or promotional announcements of evening shows. What can we do?

Answer: Complain loudly to the station and the network. Several times during daytime programs, one Boston station ran a promo for Hitchcock's movie *The Birds,* showing the final horrifying scenes of hundreds of birds pecking at a child. Before a recent evening children's special, another station showed a scene of a woman being strangled as the promo for a late night movie. Hundreds of children who tuned in early for the special saw one of the most violent scenes from the movie. There is no excuse for such thoughtless programming. First, deal with your children's reactions and help them to feel comfortable. Then call the station and complain. Then write a letter to the station with one copy to the network with which it is affiliated and one copy to the Federal Communications Commission (see Resource Directory for addresses).

ACT PRESCRIBES TENDER LOVING CARE FOR CHILDREN'S TV TROUBLES

In response to growing concern from medical professionals and parents about the effects of television on young children, Action for Children's Television has developed a set of guidelines in the form of an attractive poster called "Treat TV with T.L.C. (Tender Loving Care)." (See Figure 3.)

ACT's colorful poster is designed to raise specific questions about the content and quality of TV programming and advertising, including the portrayal of women and cultural minorities,

Figure 3

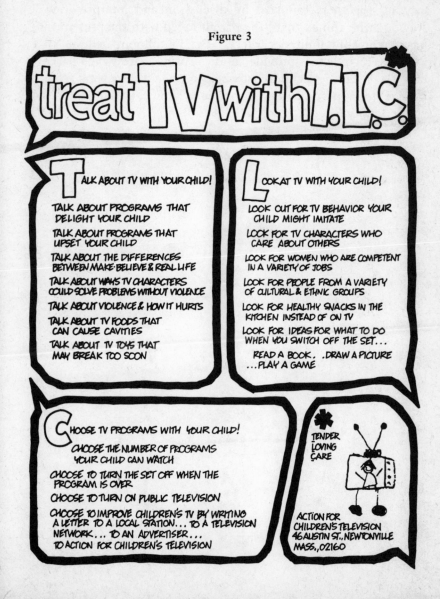

the promotion of foods that may be harmful to a child's health, the use of violence as a technique to solve interpersonal problems, and the difference between fantasy and reality.

Noted pediatric specialist Dr. Richard Feinbloom, author of the *Child Health Encyclopedia,* urges families "to do more viewing together, followed by discussion and interpretation." Although he thinks that "the parent faced with the present fare has regrettably limited choices," Dr. Feinbloom believes that "the ACT guidelines provide an ideal springboard which parents can use with their children to help change TV viewing from a passive to a participatory experience which is shared by the whole family."[1]

NOTE

[1] Action for Children's Television press release, May 18, 1976.

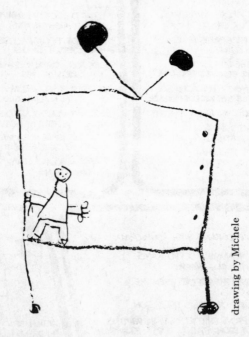

drawing by Michele

Television
and the Classroom

Since children learn from everything they watch, all TV viewing is an education for them. However, teachers and others involved in education have an extra dimension with which to reach children. In schools, television is virtually controlled by the teacher and can, therefore, be examined more objectively. There are two aspects of TV and in-school education that are growing in importance.

MEDIA IN THE SCHOOLS

Films and videotape, sound cassettes, and photographs are becoming part of our children's vocabulary at an earlier and earlier age. Some elementary-school children have already had the experience of making their own movies and TV programs, while others may have been taken on a tour of a local television station. Teachers have found that the challenge of using the new media in the classroom is usually eminently worth the trouble of learning about them. An excellent source of information in this area is the Center for Understanding Media in New York, which provides workshops for teachers interested in learning how to use special film and videotapes.

Teachers also use educational TV programs in class. There is a wide range of in-school programming, on almost all subjects, provided by such groups as National Instructional Television. These groups often provide accompanying teachers' booklets and follow-up material based on a specific curriculum. (See "Television and Education" in Resource Directory.) In addition, educational programming for in-school use is frequently shown on public television stations during the school day.

There have been some interesting experiments along those lines. In one of them, an unusual reading program involving 900 inner-city public school students in Philadelphia, children watch a videotaped program while following the written script provided for them before the class. The results show an amazing enthusiasm for reading from children who used to be bored in class, as well as incidental benefits, such as students wanting to learn typing in order to write their own scripts. Many areas have regular in-school TV programs. A typical schedule from the Division of Instructional Television in Owings Mills, Maryland, shows the range and diversity of available series. (See Figure 4 for a complete schedule for April 1978.)

At the same time, teachers have found it helpful to take advantage of programs watched by children outside of school. Programs can be linked to a subject they are studying or research projects can grow out of an issue raised on a TV show. Some teachers encourage careful monitoring of programs. Students watch specific programs and look for examples of such things as sexism and racism. One teacher asks her class to watch an early evening series, and the following day encourages questions about the show—for whom it was designed, why the characters were chosen, what the story is about, the reason for the program. In discussions like these, children can begin to analyze their viewing and to understand the necessity for critical evaluation of what they watch.

Television is increasingly being seen as a "dandy tool" to help overwhelmed teachers meet the individual learning needs of young people. For instance, Virginia Biggy, professor of education at the University of Lowell (Massachusetts) and head of the American-Canadian study team that investigated the state of instruction in the essential learning skills, told ACT:

Children understand it. They watch it for interminable lengths of time on their own. They acquire information from it. . . . Television can present five or six different approaches to the same content in one program. It can also provide several different levels at which the material is introduced and reviewed.

For example, in a minute or two a concept can be presented at the level appropriate for reaching the entire age group. Then, in the next minute or so, the examples for reviewing and applying the concept can be alternately very easy, slightly more difficult, and extremely sophisticated to meet the needs of those children who are a cut or two above the common.

Use of television as a major resource will provide time for the teacher to stand back and watch children react to instruction. Teachers can get immediate feedback and make the most of it in their planning. The opportunity to observe students at work and to make teacher-type decisions about how much more review and the like a child needs is really at the heart of the concept of the management role of the teacher.

Acknowledging public concern about basic skills teaching in the schools today, Dr. Biggy explores the enormity of the teacher's task. "It's overwhelming," she says, "merely to have to decide which of an assortment of techniques, materials, and strategies to use with which child." Television, she says, will give the teacher more time to make such decisions, and clearer insights on which to base them.

Dr. Biggy asserts that television can make its presentations "in a most vivid and effective way," with variety and relevance to children's lives. It would be "a real pity" if we did not use it to help teach the fundamentals.

"We've tried every other approach except for sending messages in bottles." Dr. Biggy concludes, "Getting at the teaching of essential skills by another route, namely television, is absolutely necessary."[1]

A HANDS-ON APPROACH

A large number of school systems now have video equipment which students use to make their own television programs. These may range from a simple video report on an ecology outing to a full-length production of a play.

In New York state, an experimental program designed to help disadvantaged elementary-school children improve their reading abilities encouraged them to make their own television programs. Known as GERIS (Graphic Expression Reading Improvement System) it uses a three-camera videotape system; the youngsters pick a topic, do research, produce graphics, write a script, practice reading the script, make a preliminary tape of the show, evaluate it, and then record a final tape. The $8,000

Figure 4
Services of the Maryland State Department of Education, Division of Instructional Television*

Telecast Schedule: First Semester

TIME	MONDAY	TUESDAY	WEDNESDAY	THURSDAY	FRIDAY
8:00	8:00-8:30 Basic Education: Teaching the Adult	8:00-830 Teaching Children with Special Needs	8:00-8:30 Teaching Children with Special Needs	8:00-8:30 Basic Education: Teaching the Adult	8:00-8:30 Teaching Children with Special Needs
8:30	MARYLAND CENTER PROGRAMMING				
9:00	9:00-9:30 Calculus (1) 9:30-9:45 Out of Order 9:45-9:50 Interlude (5 min.) 9:50-10:10 Images and Things	9:00-9:30 Ripples 9:15-9:45 American History (Oct. 7-Jan. 13) Children of the World (Jan. 20-Feb. 24) 9:45-10:00 Do You Get the Message?	9:00-9:30 Calculus (2) 9:30-9:45 Numbers Game I 9:45-10:00 Uncle Smiley (Oct. 7-Nov. 18) Elementary Consumer Education (Nov. 25-Dec. 9) The Real World of Insects (Dec. 16-Jan. 20) Basic Ecology (Jan. 27-Mar. 3)	9:00-9:15 'Way to Go (Oct. 7-Nov. 4) All About You (Nov. 11-May 19) 9:15-9:30 Numbers Game II 9:30-9:45 Inside/Out 9:45-10:00 Why/1975	9:00-9:15 Out of Order 9:15-9:30 Let's All Sing 9:30-9:50 Comparative Geography (Oct. 7-Dec. 2) Stories Without Words (Dec. 9-Jan. 27) 9:50-10:10 Music of America
10:00	10:10-10:25 The Song Bag 10:25-10:40 Whatcha Gonna Do? (Oct. 7-Dec. 2) Dignity of Work (Dec. 9-Feb. 3) 10:40-11:00 Ready? Set ... Go!	10:00-10:15 Elementary Mathematics (Oct. 7-April 7) 10:15-10:30 Exploring the World of Science (1) 10:30-10:45 Primary Art 10:45-11:00 The Real World of Insects (Oct. 7-Oct. 28) Becoming Me (Nov. 4-Feb. 3)	10:00-10:15 Stepping into Melody 10:15-10:30 Numbers Game II 10:30-10:45 Animals and Such 10:45-11:00 Why/1975	10:00-10:15 Exploring the World of Science (2) 10:15-10:30 Out of Order 10:30-10:45 The Real World of Insects (Oct. 7-Oct. 28) Becoming Me (Nov. 4-Feb. 3) 10:45-11:00 Let's All Sing	10:10-10:25 Numbers Game I 10:25-10:30 Interlude (5 min.) 10:30-11:00 American History (Oct. 7-Jan. 13) Children of the World (Jan. 20-Feb. 24)
11:00	11:00-11:30 The Electric Company	11:00-11:30 The Electric Company	11:00-11:30 The Electric Company	11:00-11:30 The Electric Company	11:00-11:30 The Electric Company
	11:30-11:50 Comparative Geography (Oct. 7-Dec. 2) Stories Without Words (Dec. 9-Jan. 27) 11:50-12:05 'Way To Go (Oct. 7-Nov. 4) All About You (Nov. 11-May 19)	11:30-11:45 Whatcha Gonna Do? (Oct. 7-Dec. 2) Dignity of Work (Dec. 9-Feb. 3) 11:45-12:00 Inside/Out	11:30-11:45 The Real World of Insects (Oct. 7-Oct. 28) Becoming Me (Nov. 4-Feb. 3) 11:45-12:00 Out of Order	11:30-11:45 Elementary Mathematics 11:45-12:00 Why/1975	11:30-12:00 Matter of Fact
12:00	12:05-12:35 Calculus (1) 12:35-12:45 Interlude (10 min.) 12:45-1:00 Stepping into Melody	12:00-12:15 The Song Bag 12:15-12:45 Matter of Fact 12:45-1:00 Numbers Game II	12:00-12:05 Interlude (5 min.) 12:05-12:35 Calculus (2) 12:35-12:50 Do You Get the Message? 12:50-1:00 Interlude (10 min.)	12:00-12:15 Primary Art 12:15-12:30 Uncle Smiley (Oct. 7-Nov. 18) Elementary Consumer Education (Nov. 25-Dec. 9) The Real World of Insects (Dec. 16-Jan. 20) Basic Ecology (Jan. 27-Mar. 3) 12:30-12:50 Comparative Geography (Oct. 7-Dec. 2) Stories Without Words (Dec. 9-Jan. 27) 12:50-1:10 Music of America	12:00-12:15 Stepping into Melody 12:15-12:30 Why/1975 12:30-12:50 Comparative Geography (Oct. 7-Dec. 2) Stories Without Words (Dec. 9-Jan. 27) 12:50-1:00 Interlude (10 min.)

Telecast Schedule: First Semester

TIME	MONDAY	TUESDAY	WEDNESDAY	THURSDAY	FRIDAY
1:00	1:00–1:15 Exploring the World of Science (1) 1:15–1:30 Animals and Such (Oct. 7–Jan. 20) Matter and Motion (Jan. 27–May 19) 1:30–1:45 Elementary Mathematics 1:45–2:00 Uncle Smiley (Oct. 7–Nov. 18) Elementary Consumer Education (Nov. 25–Dec. 9) The Real World of Insects (Dec. 16–Jan. 20) Basic Ecology (Jan. 27–Mar. 3)	1:00–1:20 Ready? Set . . . Go! 1:20–1:35 Numbers Game I 1:35–1:50 'Way To Go (Oct. 7–Nov. 4) All About You (Nov. 11–May 19) 1:50–2:10 Music of America	1:00–1:15 Why/1975 1:15–1:30 Let's All Sing 1:30–1:45 Primary Art 1:45–2:00 Out of Order	1:10–1:25 Ripples 1:25–1:30 Interlude (5 min.) 1:30–1:45 Do You Get the Message? 1:45–2:00 The Song Bag	1:00–1:15 Ripples 1:15–1:35 Images and Things 1:35–1:40 Interlude (5 min.) 1:40–1:55 Out of Order 1:55–2:00 Interlude (5 min.)
2:00	2:00–2:30 American History (Oct. 7–Jan. 13) Children of the World (Jan. 20–Feb. 24) 2:30–3:00 Matter of Fact	2:10–2:40 Matter of Fact 2:40–3:00 Images and Things	2:00–2:20 Ready? Set . . . Go! 2:20–2:30 Interlude (10 min.) 2:30–3:00 American History (Oct. 7–Jan. 13) Children of the World (Jan. 20–Feb. 24)	2:00–2:30 American History (Oct. 7–Jan. 13) Children of the World (Jan. 20–Feb. 24) 2:30–3:00 Matter of Fact	2:00–2:15 Exploring the World of Science (2) 2:15–2:30 Inside/Out 2:30–2:45 Animals and Such (Oct. 7–Jan. 22) Matter and Motion (Jan. 29–May 19) 2:45–3:00 Whatcha Gonna Do? (Oct. 7–Dec. 2) Dignity of Work (Dec. 9–Feb. 3)
3:00	MARYLAND CENTER PROGRAMMING				
6:00		6:00–6:30 Teaching Children with Special Needs 6:30–7:00 Basic Education: Teaching the Adult		6:00–6:30 Teaching Children with Special Needs 6:30–7:00 Basic Education: Teaching the Adult	6:00–6:30 GED

*Reprinted with permission.

units, which are currently in use in over a dozen school systems, include three cameras and the videotape.

Administrators say that the program has doubled the reading scores of many of the youngsters. One official noted: "The program capitalizes on the importance television plays in the lifestyle of today's child, and makes children want to read, because they need to read so that they can produce a short television show on their own."

Bringing Prime Time to the Classroom

One unique nonprofit organization is working to encourage teachers to use prime time television programs as part of the secondary school curriculum. Begun in Chicago in 1970, Prime Time School Television (PTST) distributes education materials to schoolteachers across the country designed to change "passive viewing into an active educational experience."

PTST devises curriculum aids which tell teachers about program content and suggest important themes for discussion. The units provide supplementary background information and include a list of suggested readings. PTST allows teachers to add TV-based lesson plans to history, English, or government courses. PTST describes its long-range goal:

"By encouraging teachers to develop a sense of critical viewing in their students, PTST thinks the teachers in turn will be able to influence television programming by creating a demand for better quality programming."

Because of the popularity of TV crime dramas, PTST recently developed an innovative packet of materials entitled *Television, Police, and the Law*. It deals with some important issues:

1. Are students receiving false impressions of police officers from television dramas?
2. Are constitutional guidelines for police action misrepresented on television?
3. Do seemingly easy solutions for baffling crimes mold the police into super heroes?
4. Are crime dramas fostering unreal expectations of law enforcement officers?

The packet includes a student reader containing articles and court cases, logs for monitoring use of force, constitutional awareness, and crime-solving techniques, and a teacher guide for additional activities. Recommended for courses in social studies, language arts, law, media and communications, and career education in grades seven through twelve, the unit encourages students to view television police shows more critically. Moreover, teachers can discuss points of law with examples that come directly from a student's TV experience.

TV STIMULATES READING

One unexpected reaction to the increased use of dramatizations of books for children has been increased demand for these books at libraries and bookstores. "As soon as there's a television show about a book, we get a tremendous number of children coming in and asking for it," said one librarian. A bookshop salesperson noted that the recent series based on the Hardy Boys and Nancy Drew adventures have dramatically increased the demand for the books, which still entertain children today, years after their original publication.

Educators have begun to take advantage of this phenomenon. One in-school reading program about books, "Cover to Cover," from WETA in Washington, D.C., often introduces a book in dramatized form, stopping in the middle and urging young viewers to find the book for themselves and learn how it ends. "We always have to tell school libraries what books we're going to present so that they can make sure they have copies," said a production assistant on the series, "because there's always a run on the book after we've shown the program."

Using Television To Read

The idea of using television as a reading aid came from Philadelphia—perhaps sparked by the success of CTW's "Sesame Street" and "Electric Company" with younger children.

The Philadelphia Reading Program was initiated in 1970 by Dr. Michael McAndrew, a reading specialist, and Dr. Michael Marcase, now superintendent of the Philadelphia schools. The program stimulates students' interest in reading by providing scripts of upcoming television programs to young viewers so that they can read along as they watch. The TV dramatization of Joseph Lash's *Eleanor and Franklin* in January 1976 provides an outstanding example of the project's success. With cooperation from ABC and financial support from IBM (the show's sponsor), the *Philadelphia Inquirer* published the entire script in a special supplement distributed the Friday before the program was aired. An estimated 84 percent of youngsters in the target group (grades seven through twelve), watched the show with their families while following it in the printed script. In class the next week, the majority showed an obvious interest in the drama, as well as in the reading experience itself. Dr. McAndrew commented:

"The kids not only bought out the stores and borrowed the libraries out of the one book, but they wanted to read Lash's other books as well . . . When they got into Lash, they wanted to taste more of his writing style, his use of language. The reading experience *itself* got to them. If TV can do that to a kid, TV deserves a lot of applause."[2]

Another interesting study, begun in 1971, is described in an article in *ACT News*. (See Figure 5.)

"Vanishing Shadow" in Florida

In Jacksonville, Florida, the 1934 movie serial, "The Vanishing Shadow," is used to help 18,000 sixth- and seventh-grade students with their reading.

The series is broadcast every week, Monday through Thursday evening, on WJXT, the Post-Newsweek station in Jacksonville. Children are given scripts of the show and told to watch the program.

The next day in class they read the script and use it to discuss and act out the episode. Teachers also use puzzles and word games related to the episodes as a means of building vocabulary. Sometimes students are asked to write alternative scripts and act them out.

The twelve episodes of the serial center on the rivalry between the hero, Stanley Stanfield, an electrical engineer, and the villain, Wade Barnett. Each episode ends with Stanfield in

Figure 5

Dual audio concept boosts video value

Four years ago, the Philadelphia Board of Education was funded by the federal government to determine whether radio and television could be effectively combined into a single educational medium for children. An article in the Summer, 1975 issue of the *Journal of Communication* by three directors of the project provides some interesting answers and raises more questions about the future of Dual Audio Television.

In "Dual Audio Television Goes Public," authors Terry Borton, Leonard Belasco, and A. Rae Williams describe dual audio as the simultaneous broadcast of a popular children's television program and a coordinated FM radio supplement. The dual audio narrator, they explain, "does not talk while the TV characters are talking, or during commercials, but waits until there are pauses in the TV dialogue to make his comments. He uses the TV program material as examples for instruction in basic skills, particularly vocabulary development."

In April, 1974, WKBS-TV and WUHY-FM cooperated with the Philadelphia School Board's Office of Curriculum and Instruction in the first publicly announced broadcast of dual audio television using "Gilligan's Island." The article reports the results of a survey of over 250 second through fifth graders from seven schools in the Philadelphia area to determine whether the dual audio concept could contribute to measurable improvement in the children's vocabulary scores.

The most significant gains, it was found, were made by second and third graders, who increased their previous ratings "by an average of 5% (equivalent to one word) for each day listened."

After the initial findings were confirmed in a followup study conducted among children who watched a dual audio version of "The Flintstones," project directors Borton, Belasco, and Williams concluded that "such a pattern of evidence suggests that dual audio should be an effective means of supplemental mass education."

Although the parents of the children tested were unanimous in their opinion that dual audio was "a good idea," there was no attempt to ascertain the reactions of the children's teachers. The possibility remains, therefore, that the young participants in this unprecedented experiment might have achieved even greater success had their classroom sessions been tailored to reinforce the spoken explanation of the dual audio narrator. □[3]

dire circumstances from which he miraculously escapes the following day.

Dr. John T. Gunning, Jacksonville's superintendent of schools, stated that the cost of the project was low, and that the children were excited. "It seems," said Gunning, "that television has capabilities for instruction that haven't begun to be tapped yet." The success of the Jacksonville project led Post-Newsweek to expand the project to Greenwich, Connecticut, Benton Harbor, Michigan, and Brooklyn and Mount Vernon in New York.

Post-Newsweek vice-president Ray Hubbard, whose stations initiated the project, commented: "It is a dumb serial, but it honest-to-God works and nobody knows why. The kids started reading like crazy. These were mainly inner-city kids who had not been reading."

CBS Television Reading Program

In 1977 CBS Television began a television reading program designed to motivate children to read more. Schools are given full scripts of selected television dramas before broadcast. Teachers are given reading enrichment guides based on the dramas, intended to spark class discussion on the values in the story as well as to suggest additional activities. The network has set up a central office to help CBS affiliates and local schoolboards introduce the program into different areas.

When the script of *A Circle of Children* was printed by a St. Louis newspaper, teachers questioned after the broadcast of the program rated the experiment as "an outstanding and worthwhile educational experience" and recommended expanding the program.

Helping Poor Readers

In Wilmington, Delaware, a project involving more than 750 eighth- and ninth-grade students has used video cassettes of programs like "Gilligan's Island," "Fat Albert," and "The Rookies" to help improve reading skills.

"What we're doing is taking television, something the kids are interested in and involved in, and then using it to teach them something they need to know—reading. How else do you get eighth- and ninth-grade students interested in learning to read when they have missed the boat for so long?" said Wilmington school administrator Morton Witlin. Wilmington has obtained a $33,900 federal grant to test the success of the program in the city's schools. One eighth-grade teacher commented: "It's very motivating. The students really enjoy having something they can identify with." Her class has studied "Brian's Song" and "The Autobiography of Miss Jane Pittman," as well as series like "The Rookies."

CONSUMER EDUCATION IN THE SCHOOLS

Television is the first medium to treat all children as miniature consumers and to advertise to them on their own programs. Parents and teachers, therefore, need to encourage children to cope with advertising pressures and to learn about value and prices. In-school groups can examine all aspects of advertising directed to children, and teachers can show children the different techniques used in the commercials directed to them.

The Loyola University Communications Education work texts dealing with "Persuasion" and "Mass Media" are excellent basic materials for a lively approach to this topic for older children. Teachers can help younger children to understand the concepts of advertising and the reasons why some ads might be misleading. Some teachers encourage children to prepare their own commercials and examine them. One teacher in New Hampshire organized his class to file a complaint with a local television station which had advertised a simple toy that didn't work the way the ad had promised, after several children in the class had bought it. Several law schools encourage students to become involved in actual communications actions and to do research and file legal briefs on them.

TV PROGRAM INFORMATION

TV Guide: Independent weekly magazine giving full listings and additional articles and information.

Newspapers: Weekly schedules in Sunday newspapers in many cities. See also daily listings.

American Educator: American Federation of Teachers, AFL-CIO, 11 Dupont Circle, N.W., Washington, D.C. 20036. Regular TV supplement includes guides to upcoming programming.

Prime Time School Television: 100 North LaSalle Street, Chicago, Ill. 60602.

Teachers' Guide to Television: 745 Fifth Avenue, New York, N.Y. 10021. Twice-yearly magazine with background and additional material about special programs.

Children's TV Workshop: 1 Lincoln Plaza, New York, N.Y. 10023. Can provide follow-up materials for "Sesame Street" and "Electric Company" or direct you to regional information centers.

State educational agencies or public television stations can also provide lists of in-school programs available locally.

NOTES

[1] Reprinted with permission of Action for Children's Television.

[2] Maureen Harmonay, "Reading: The Mass Media as Motivation," *re:act* 7: 1 & 2 (Fall 1977), p. 8.

[3] *ACT News,* Fall 1975. Reprinted with permission of Action for Children's Television.

Violence and the FCC

In medicine a basic principle is, "First do no harm!" Television might well adopt this as its first principle for children's programing. It might meet that goal by insisting that those creative people who devise and produce programs for children become thoroughly familiar with the knowledge which already exists about child growth and development.[1]

While it is difficult to state exactly what effect watching violent programs on television will have upon individual children, it seems inconsistent with research to claim—as many broadcasters do—that it has no effect at all. Parents should watch some of the programs that their children see and make their own decisions about what to allow or ban.

The real question about violence on television is *why* it should be a part of children's programming in the first place. After all, there are a million and one other things in the world that could be subjects for children's shows. However, since there is a great deal of violence on television, much research has been conducted in this area.

Studies prepared for the Surgeon General's Scientific Advisory Committee on Television and Social Behavior found that children's cartoons were the most violent of all programs examined. Dr. George Gerbner of the Annenberg School of Communications, University of Pennsylvania, stated:

"It is . . . clear that children watching Saturday morning cartoons had the least chance of escaping violence or of avoiding the heaviest . . . saturation of violence on all television." Dr. Gerbner found that "the average cartoon hour had nearly six times the violence rate of the average adult television drama hour."[2]

As an example, Dr. John Schowalter, of the Yale Child Psychiatry Unit and the Yale School of Medicine, describes what befell the coyote in a six-minute segment of "Roadrunner," which he considers one of the least frightening of the cartoons for preschool children:

In minute one, a cannon blew his head off; in minute two he was pushed under a boulder; in minute three, he fell a long, long way to plop in a puff of dust to the canyon floor; in minute four, he fell again and was later blown up; in minute five, he was run over by a truck and later crushed by a rock; and in minute six he was run over yet again to total eight alleged deaths in six minutes.[3]

STUDIES ON VIOLENCE

Television in the Afterschool Hours, an ACT-commissioned study conducted by Dr. F. Earle Barcus of Boston University in 1975, examined, among other things, the amount of violence on television seen by children between 3:00 and 6:00 P.M.

Ten-Station Analysis

The following ten stations were selected for detailed analysis: WNEW, New York; WDCA, Washington, D.C.; WUTV, Buffalo; WKBD, Detroit; WVTV, Milwaukee; WDRB, Louisville; WYAH, Norfolk-Portsmouth; WTCG, Atlanta; KSTW, Seattle-Tacoma; KTXZ, Sacramento-Stockton.

The ACT monitoring study noted that "of the total audience viewing the thirty hours of programming studied, almost two-thirds, on the average, are children. . . . In eight of the ten markets, 50 percent or more of the audience were children aged two to eleven."

In his analysis of violent programming content, Dr. Barcus concluded that "if the overall level of violence has been reduced in all of children's television, as claimed by the newer network productions, it is far from true for independent station programs."[4]

Overall, continued the ACT report, "more than six of ten stories contained some observable act of violence, and about three in ten were 'saturated' with violent acts. These latter programs were based on little else than violent action to sustain the story. Cartoon comedy and the older action-adventure programs account for most of the violent episodes."

Although violence was most often directed at human characters, deaths do not occur frequently. There were injuries in about one-quarter of all the stories.

To demonstrate the study's definition of violence, Dr. Barcus included the following items as "examples" of the kind of violence he and his associates found in their research. (A complete listing of Dr. Barcus's sample is found in Appendix B).

Examples of Violence in the Stories

Human Violence With Weapons:
Humorous Contexts (Comedy Drama)

"Shish-ka-Bugs" (Bugs Bunny)—Cook threatens Bugs Bunny with a meat cleaver (cook is human).

"Rapid Romance" (Ricochet Rabbit)—Guns are fired; their bullets turn into mallets that hit Rabbit over the head.

"Zero Hero" (Touche Turtle and Dum Dum)—Touche stabs gorilla with sword.

Violence Without Weapons:
Humorous Context (Comedy Drama)

"Hong Kong Phooey"—"In-nose" man attempts to drown brothers of mystery man.

"Bachelor Buttons" (Wally Gator)—Ella Gator punches Wally, grabs his tail, and smashes him, then does the same to a lion.

Action-Adventure Drama

"Else When" (Land of the Lost)—Monsters try to strangle Dad and Will, then tie them up.

Natural Violence
Humorous Context

"Fulton's Folly" (U.S. of Archie)—Two explosions in science lab, several ships sink.

"Hook, Line and Stinker" (Roadrunner)—Coyote is struck by lightning.

Action-Adventure Drama
"Run Joe Run"—Fire results in child being burned.
"Shazam"—Rattlesnake poisons Danny and he is trapped by falling rock slide.

What the Research Shows

Dr. George Comstock, of the Newhouse School of Communications at Syracuse University, delivered a paper at the National Homicide Symposium in San Francisco in 1976 that gave a succinct overview of what we have learned about the effects of television violence.

Since the early 1950s there have been no less than seven congressional hearings focused on the issue of television violence. Most of these have been major Senate hearings conducted by such well-known figures as Kefauver and Pastore. The recent hearings conducted in Los Angeles and other cities by Congressman Lionel Van Deerlin would bring the total to eight. In addition, media violence was the subject of a voluminous staff report to the National Commission on the Causes and Prevention of Violence in 1969, and in 1972 the Surgeon General's study of television violence concluded with the publication of five volumes reporting on $1 million in new research and the interpretative report of a specially assembled advisory committee.

The major question addressed by these inquiries is whether violent television entertainment contributes to greater aggressiveness on the part of young viewers. The same question has been addressed in various ways by numerous social and behavioral science studies.

Dr. Comstock believes that further research is needed in this area, but he does conclude:

Young children may imitate violence and presumably other acts they see portrayed on television. Apparently, these children, in seeing acts on television that are new or untypical of them, become better able or more likely to perform them at a later time. The notion that they can be thought of as adding these acts to their repertoire of possible behavior is supported by the finding that children who do not voluntarily imitate portrayed behavior can do so when asked. The theory that has been developed to explain this phenomenon is called "observational learning theory," and it holds that persons can learn or become more proficient at performing acts simply by observing them either in real life or in a movie or on television. Actual performance, of course, is contingent on a variety of circumstances. . . .[5]

Numerous studies illustrate Dr. Comstock's point. An independent study sponsored as one of a series by the National Institute of Mental Health showed that the behavior of preschool children changed for the worse when they were shown violent television programs and improved when they were exposed to "socially constructive" ones. The study was conducted by Dr. Aletha Stein and Dr. Lynette Friedrich, both assistant professors of human development at Pennsylvania State University, with the assistance of Dr. Fred W. Vondracek.

In this study, a group of preschool children was exposed, over a four-week period, to twelve programs which were classified as "aggressive" (including "Superman" and "Batman") or "prosocial" (including "Mister Rogers' Neighborhood"). The viewers of the aggressive programs displayed increased physical or verbal aggression or both. Those who watched the prosocial programs were said to have improved their observance of rules, tolerance of delays, and persistence at tasks. A third group, shown programs regarded as "neutral" in effect, exhibited reactions falling well between the two extremes.

Dr. John E. Schowalter has stated: "It is clear that the children most at risk of being harmed by inappropriate programming are those under the age of five or six," but "I have also been consulted by older children whose anxieties or phobias were intertwined with the frightening TV shows that they have seen."

Dr. Schowalter believes that the violence and death on children's shows "probably make it harder for them to mourn actual deaths." To the argument that these are natural and should therefore be part of children's TV, he answers:

Unfortunately, violence and death are often portrayed in the most unnatural forms and as the most obvious, if not the only, way to settle personal problems. Invariably absent are the damage, pain, grief, mourning, destruction, and other consequences of violence in real life. . . . It is not that violence and death should never be shown on TV but that writers and producers of children's shows should take more into account what is already known about children's development.[6]

Some broadcasters allege that parents are shielding children from reality when they attack programs that glorify violence and depict killing. In fact, they suggest that it is a healthy educational process for children to be exposed to such incidents, preparing them for adulthood. It is up to each parent to determine whether programs are educational or frightening for his child.

You should examine carefully adult programs that contain violence or killing before you decide whether you want your child to watch them. News programs, which often contain real life violence, should be considered in the same way, since they can confuse and upset a young child. Also, it is often a great help for a child to watch the news with adults, who can explain what is going on.

In a study for the Surgeon General's report *Television and Social Behavior,* Thomas F. Baldwin and Colby Lewis interviewed script writers and producers for adult programs. One writer admitted that violence in programming was an inevitable consequence of the commercial broadcasting system, and said: "We aren't going to get rid of violence until we get rid of advertisers. The advertiser wants something with which to get the audience. Violence equals excitement equals ratings."[7]

There is violence on children's television because it sells products. Broadcasters and advertisers know that children will watch a fast, action-packed cartoon in preference to most other programs, which is why so many such cartoons exist; they get high ratings and sell products. One mother said: "If I were telling my children a story and two men started fighting in the corner of the room, it would be very hard to stop them from watching the fight."

In 1972, at hearings before a Senate committee, all the members of the Commission on Television and Social Behavior admitted during questioning by Senator John Pastore that there was a causal link between children who watched television violence and some aggressive behavior.

Television clearly seems to have a cumulative effect, resulting from watching not one program but a consistent pattern of programs. Parents have always known that television shows have a direct effect on children's behavior in some cases, since they have seen them act out TV-inspired situations and characters. Advertisers too are well aware that TV has a persuasive effect, and are only too willing to spend money taking advantage of it. Ironically, broadcasters consistenly claim that nobody can prove specific effects of violent programming, while they never doubt the persuasive effects of the commercials shown between these programs.

1976—A MOST VIOLENT TV SEASON

One of the results of the concern about the effects of TV violence in the late 1960s was the setting up of a Television Violence Index. Dr. George Gerbner and Dr. Larry Gross of the Annenberg School of Communications, University of Pennsylvania, devised a system of monitoring television programs and measuring the number of violent incidents on the air. Each year since 1967 they have published a *Violence Index*, which measures the amount of violence to which television audiences have been exposed from watching prime time series, late evening shows, dramatic programs, as well as weekend daytime network television.

In March 1977, they released their *Violence Profile No. 8*, which was based on the examination of samples of programs in the fall of 1976:

TV violence increased sharply in all categories, including "family viewing" and children's programs on all three networks. The increase resulted in the highest Violence Index on record. The only score that comes close to the current record of 203.6 was the score of 198.7 in 1967, the year of turmoil that led to the establishment of the Eisenhower Violence Commission and our TV Violence Index.[8]

Gerbner and Gross have carried out many studies to find out if people who watch more than four hours of television a day have different responses to general daily experiences than those who watch less than four hours a day. Their research has led them to believe that people who watch more than four hours—heavy viewers—are often more fearful of everyday life, have an exaggerated idea of the dangers in the world, have misconceptions about the number of policemen, the role of women, and other value-based ideas that are affected by television's presentations, and such misconceptions are only alleviated in cases where newspapers or news magazines are regularly read.

From 1975 and 1976 on, there has been growing concern about the effect of televised violence on our children. The National Congress of Parents and Teachers (PTA) organized a major campaign to focus attention on the issue. They held hearings in ten cities where broadcasters, researchers, and other experts spoke on the topic and answered questions from the audience. Although there was no legislative action attached to these meetings, they served to emphasize public concern with TV violence and to draw the attention of those most closely connected with children's viewing to the effects of violence on the screen.

The prestigious *New England Journal of Medicine* polled over 1500 physicians concerning the impact of TV violence on children. Drs. Timothy Johnson and Murray Feingold presented the responses to network representatives. They noted:

We maintain that the burden of proof that television violence does no harm lies with those who introduce it into our society. Advertisers and networks will respond if continuous public pressure is maintained.[9]

THE FAMILY HOUR

In response to growing public pressure to reduce TV violence, the networks, cooperating with the National Association of Broadcasters, instituted the "Family Viewing Hour" in the fall of 1975. A public-relations effort to assure viewers that programming aired between 7:00 and 9:00 P.M. would be "suitable" for family viewing, this network ploy was overturned by the courts in the fall of 1976. Federal District Judge Warren J. Ferguson ruled that the family hour violated First Amendment guarantees of freedom of speech. ACT's Peggy Charren agreed:

ACT is concerned about the amount of unrelenting violence and senseless brutality which characterizes so many of the networks' prime time programs. But ACT believes that the family hour concept operated primarily as a public-relations effort designed to dissuade people from exerting meaningful efforts toward the improvement of children's television. . . . The Family Hour, rather than encouraging worthwhile alternatives to the status quo, has been invoked to crush creativity and justify the fact that children, the supposed benefactors of this concept, are still the audience offered the least amount of programming designed for their age or interests. . . . Restricting options is not the way to create meaningful diversity on TV.[10]

HOW TO REDUCE VIOLENCE ON TELEVISION

Reducing the amount of violence children see on television remains a complicated and, so far, unsolved problem. How can we protect our children from gratuitous and meaningless violence without threatening the broadcaster's right to freedom of speech? How can we protect our children, but still encourage broadcasters to air thoughtful programming for adults, which will, at times, include violence because it is a serious social problem?

Action for Children's Television was formed because of concern about excessive violence on children's television, but the organization recognizes that we cannot make all of television programming appropriate for young children, nor would we want to. Jean Johnson, ACT's Resource Director, comments:

ACT has made children's television an issue of importance for parents, teachers, child professionals, and the public at large. But since its inception and throughout its eight years as an advocate for children and their parents, ACT has repeatedly and emphatically rejected the all too easy role of censor on behalf of the nation's children. ACT has encouraged needed reforms in the area of children's broadcasting without threatening the First Amendment rights of the broadcaster. ACT believes that no special interest group, ACT included, should determine which television programs are placed on the air. Instead, ACT has called for more diversity in children's television and pointed out the need for programs designed for specific age levels rather than directed to the entire audience of children in the two- to eleven-year age span. ACT has never provided broadcasters with a list of criteria which would produce a "good children's television show," realizing that such a manifesto would discourage, rather than encourage, the creativity, commitment, and sensitivity needed to improve programming for children.[11]

ACT's analysis of children's television practices convinced the organization that as long as broadcasters believed that violent programs were the easiest way to get the highest share of the ratings, and thus the most advertising dollars, they would continue to schedule violence for children.

In the long term, the only way to reduce the violence on television would be to take children's programming out of the ratings system and make it a public service area. This would mean that there would be no commercials on children's programs, but a simple one-line underwriting message would follow the shows ("This program was brought to you by the Everything Company"). In this way, advertisers would not vie for the highest possible number of viewers, but would want to be associated with a popular but high quality show which would reflect well on the company's image. Naturally, such a step would have to be implemented in the public interest by a regulatory agency such as the Federal Communications Commission.

WHAT CAN THE FEDERAL COMMUNICATIONS COMMISSION DO?

Theoretically, the FCC can do a great deal. The six commissioners and a chairman are appointed by the president and serve a seven-year term. They and their staff are responsible for the licensing and regulation of broadcast channels in the United

States. They are committed to the concept of locally based stations serving the interests of individual communities. It is the duty of the FCC to select the best qualified local operators and to review their performance periodically to determine if they are meeting the needs of the community. The FCC grants licenses to broadcasters for three-year periods which are usually renewed almost automatically, although that was not the intention of the original mandate. The FCC has the power and the obligation to deny a license to any broadcaster who is not serving the community to the best of his or her ability.

The Communications Act of 1934 requires all stations to broadcast "in the public interest, convenience and necessity." The FCC has interpreted this provision as requiring fairness in the handling of controversial issues of public importance. To achieve such fairness, the FCC has promulgated a Fairness Doctrine which is the keystone of ethical broadcasting service.

The case of the *Red Lion Broadcasting Company* v. *the FCC* in 1969 resulted in a landmark decision with the historic assertion of the importance of broadcasting for the benefit of the public, not the convenience of the broadcaster. It stated: "It is the right of the viewers and listeners, not the right of the broadcasters, which is paramount." Much of the present activity in citizens' rights in broadcasting and in criticism of inadequate children's programming is based on this decision.

In practical terms, however, it is the broadcaster rather than the public who has ready access to the FCC. Broadcasters usually have a lawyer in Washington, and sometimes a lobbyist as well, to make sure that their interests are represented. The headquarters of the commercial broadcasting organization, the National Association of Broadcasters, is an imposing building a few blocks from the offices of the commission. In many ways, some subtle and some less subtle, the broadcaster can reach the commissioners and their staff. Broadcasters have adequate funds to cover their lobbying efforts, while most citizens' organizations, especially those of minority groups, are made up of volunteers working on a minimal budget. Pressure to bring change is time-consuming, and few citizens' groups have had the resources or the funds to compete with the affluence of the broadcasting lobby. While it should be pointed out that individual commissioners have shown outstanding commitment to the public interest, in the long run, the broadcasters' interests usually have prevailed.

FCC and Children's Television

In late 1969, the FCC announced that it wanted broadcasters to find out the needs of their communities and that it was compiling a primer on the ascertainment of community needs. ACT wrote to the FCC urging that a question on children's programs be part of the ascertainment, and was invited to meet with the commission to discuss this issue. In February 1970, five ACT members met with six of the seven commissioners in a two-hour discussion, at which ACT presented the commission with the following guidelines:

1. There shall be no sponsorship and no commercials on children's programs.

2. No performer shall be permitted to use or mention products, services, or stores by brand name during children's programs, nor shall such names be included in any way during children's programs.

3. Each station shall provide daily programming for children and in no case shall this be less than fourteen hours a week, as part of its public service requirement. Provision shall be made for programming in each of the age groups specified below, and during the time periods specified below:

   A. Preschool: Ages 2–5:   7:00 A.M.–6:00 P.M. daily
                                 7:00 A.M.–6:00 P.M. weekends

   B. Primary: Ages 6–9:   4:00 P.M.–8:00 P.M. daily
                                 8:00 A.M.–8:00 P.M. weekends

   C. Elementary: Ages 10–12: 5:00 P.M.–9:00 P.M. daily
                                 9:00 A.M.–9:00 P.M. weekends

A week later, the FCC released the guidelines in the form of a public notice, for comment, and a year later, in January 1971, the FCC initiated an inquiry into children's television.

Broadcasters, advertisers, and their lawyers filed weighty

legal arguments with the FCC. ACT turned to the public and urged them to write. The response was unprecedented in the history of the FCC. Over 100,000 letters and comments were received by the FCC from individuals, groups, and organizations representing millions of people, over 98 percent of them supporting ACT's guidelines.

In 1971, the Children's Bureau was set up at the FCC with Elizabeth Roberts as its first director. It was her initiative that motivated the hearings the FCC held on children's television in the fall of 1972 and in January 1973. Broadcasters and advertisers were represented by their lawyers and directors. Besides Action for Children's Television, representatives from a wide range of citizens' organizations also made their voices heard, including: the San Francisco Bay Area Association of Black Psychologists; the Chinese Media Committee; the National Organization for Women; the American Federation of State, County and Municipal Employees (AFL-CIO); Consumers Union; the National Association for the Education of Young Children; the National Parent-Teacher Association; HEW's Office of Child Development; and the League of United Latin American Citizens.

While the industry protested that change was impossible and that advertising never hurt anybody, the voices of the diverse citizens' groups brought up the issues of minority representation, the needs of children of different ages, and the responsibility of the broadcaster to provide some programming for the child audience.

In November 1974, after four years of debate, the FCC issued a lengthy *Report and Policy Statement on Children's Television Programs* which avoided making any rules or regulations relating to children's programming. The only legally binding change was the addition of a separate question to the license renewal form completed by every local broadcaster, relating to the quantity of children's programs aired on her or his station. In November 1975, ACT filed an unsuccessful brief appealing the FCC's decision, in the U.S. Court of Appeals in Washington, D.C. In July 1978, the FCC reopened the case by initiating an inquiry into children's television programming and advertising practices.

Broadcasters React

Although ACT's petition to the FCC did not result in rules relating to children's television, the specter of federal intervention did prompt major changes in broadcast advertising policies. The *Television Code* of the National Association of Broadcasters (NAB), a self-regulatory standard to which approximately 60 percent of the local stations subscribe, prohibited host-selling. Advertising time on Saturday morning children's programs was reduced from sixteen minutes per hour to nine and a half, and commercial time on afterschool shows dropped from sixteen minutes to twelve. In addition, the code prohibited the advertising of vitamin pills on children's shows.

While ACT applauded these steps to protect children, the group recognized that federal regulation was required. Forty percent of the television stations in the United States do not subscribe to the *Television Code,* and the NAB's ability to police broadcast practices is severely limited by the lack of a meaningful monitoring program. Warren Braren, associate director of Consumers Union and formerly manager of the New York office of the NAB Code Authority, pointed out: "The Code Authority is powerless—a pawn of the networks and its parent association, the NAB. The Code Authority director holds his position accordingly. He seeks no power and none is given to him. On any significant problem brought to the Code Authority, consensus is first sought from the networks."[12]

FIREWORKS HAZARD

The inability of the NAB code to protect children from potentially dangerous ad practices can be illustrated by ACT's experience in the summer of 1975. Although the laws in most states restrict the sale of fireworks to adults, ads for fireworks were scheduled for broadcast two weeks prior to July 4, 1975, on a Washington, D.C., station, WDCA–TV. The commercials would have been aired during a number of shows seen primarily by children, including "Bugs Bunny," "Bewitched," "Bozo's Circus," and "Superman." At that time there was no ruling within the voluntary code of the National Association of Broadcasters to stop the airing of such ads during children's programs.

Moreover, WDCA was not a code subscriber, and therefore not liable to the code's only penalty: expulsion from *Television Code* membership.

When ACT learned that the fireworks ads were planned, the station's general manager was contacted. He agreed to withdraw the ads during children's programs, but had ACT not been alerted to the problem by the American Academy of Pediatrics, there might well have been more July 4th fireworks accidents in the Washington, D.C., area than usual.

Dr. Allan B. Coleman, of the American Academy of Pediatrics, explained: "Children look on fireworks as toys, but they produce a wide variety of soft tissue injuries, eye injuries, amputations, and burns. Many of these injuries have caused permanent damage, including blindness, scarring and disfiguration, deafness and death."

ACT's quick response received kudos from parents and industry spokesmen alike. *Advertising Age*, Madison Avenue's primary trade journal, commented:

Considering the high level of consciousness that presumably exists in a city that appears to concern itself with little more than the regulation of advertising, it is hard to believe that any business or TV station in that particular market would consider such a venture. Yet this campaign, involving fifty-four spots on such programs as "Bozo's Circus" and "Bugs Bunny," might have taken place except that someone tipped off Action for Children's Television (ACT). And the station reconsidered.[13]

Later in 1975, the NAB added a regulation prohibiting the sale of fireworks directly to children on television. The industry reacted, but only after the fact.

NOTES

[1] Dr. Richard Granger, Yale Child Study Center, in *Who Is Talking to Our Children?* p.8.

[2] "Violence in Television Drama: Trends and Symbolic Function," *Television and Social Behavior*, Vol. 1, p. 36. (Washington, D.C.: 1972).

[3] *Who is Talking to Our Children?*, p. 11.

[4] F. Earle Barcus, *Television in the Afterschool Hours* (Newtonville, MA: 1975), pp. 19–21.

[5] George Comstock, *The Evidence of Television Violence* (Santa Monica, CA: 1976), p. 1; p. 10.

[6] *Who is Talking to Our Children?* p. 12.

[7] *Television and Social Behavior* (Washington, D.C.: 1972), Vol. 1, p. 314.

[8] George Gerbner and Larry Gross, *Violence Profile No. 8* (Philadelphia, PA: 1977).

[9] Murray Feingold and G. Timothy Johnson, "Television Violence—Reactions from Physicians, Advertisers and the Networks," *New England Journal of Medicine* (February 24, 1977), p. 424.

[10] *ACT News* editorial (Fall 1975).

[11] Jean Johnson, "Children's TV: The Challenge to ACT," *Top of the News* (Fall 1976), p. 66.

[12] *Action for Children's Television,* p. 96.

[13] *Advertising Age* (June 30, 1975).

The Advertising Game-Gimme Gimme Gimme

So you have carefully screened the TV programs your children are watching. You have set acceptable rules for what they can watch and when. You have limited the amount of time the set can be on. Now what?

For children watching commercial TV there is one more problem—the constant deluge of advertisements.

The only way to find children's TV programs without commercials is to turn to public TV—or turn the set off. On commercial programs children see a steady bombardment of ads for toys, cereals, candies, snack foods, and—until recently—vitamin pills.

Children currently see up to nine and a half minutes of advertising per hour on weekend children's programs, down from a high of sixteen minutes in 1970. During the week, children's daytime programs can have up to twelve minutes of advertising per hour. Several monitoring studies have found that some stations do exceed these limits and that frequent use of 30-second commercials has increased the number of ads children see each hour, although the total advertising minutes have been reduced.

Parents are well aware of the power and impact of television commercials on their children. A national probability sample of 1,230 families conducted by Yankelovich, Skelly & White for "The General Mills American Family Report, 1976–77," identified "ten major nagging problems in raising children." According to the study, 32 percent of the parents cited "children filling up with snacks between meals"; 26 percent were annoyed because "children [are] always asking for things they see advertised"; and 23 percent said they were bothered by "children watching too much television."

In the area of nutrition, the report noted, "the big controversy . . . is over snacks—with parents mentioning snacking between meals by their children as one of the major frustrations and sources of irritation."

Children are exposed to an overwhelming barrage of ads on both programs designed for their viewing and on adult programs aired at times when advertisers know children are watching. To put things in perspective, here are some key facts about children and television advertising:

The average child watches television twenty-five to thirty hours a week.

That child will watch over five hours of advertising each week.

Food advertising constitutes on the average over 60 percent of commercials directed to children.

Of the food advertised, vegetables, dairy products, and bread constitute less than 4 percent.

Sugared cereals outnumber other cereals by a margin of three to one.

Sugared cereals sold as "part of a balanced breakfast" may have as much as 60 percent sugar as an ingredient.

98 percent of the American population suffers from tooth decay.

Toys are sold with minimal product information, and warnings or caution about the use of products are seldom given, even though the product itself may sometimes include such information.

Advertisers spend over $600 million a year selling to children.

WHAT'S WRONG WITH SELLING TO CHILDREN?

In many ways, selling to children is unfair. Children are recognized as being less mature and educated than adults and, because of this, we try to protect them. Joan Ganz Cooney,

president of the Children's Television Workshop, which produces "Sesame Street" and "Electric Company," puts it this way: "If we as a total society put the interest of our children first, then we are led to the inescapable conclusion that it is terribly wrong to be pitching products at the young. It is like shooting fish in a barrel. It is grotesquely unfair."[1]

For some reason, while we don't allow teachers to sell products to children in schools, we accept selling to children on television. If a salesman rang our doorbell and said: "Hi, I'm your friendly neighborhood toy salesman and I'd like to come into your living room and show your four-year-old a few toys while you go on cooking in the kitchen. I'll just show him the toys and he can tell you what he likes," as responsible adults we'd slam the door in his face. We know that most four-year-olds couldn't cope with a fast-talking toy salesman. Yet this happens every day on commercial television. We allow salesmen into our living rooms through television and not only do we allow them on adult programs, but we allow them on programs specifically designed for very young audiences.

How Children Reason

In a speech given to the Advertising Club of Boston in November 1971, Dr. Freda Rebelsky, professor of psychology and director of the Doctoral Program in Developmental Psychology at Boston University, summarized what we have learned about children's perceptions:

Children are creatures that look somewhat like us, and we see them essentially as little adults. All recent research suggests that the sense we have that children are only quantitatively different from adults is just plain wrong. The child is an active organizer of the world. He does not see and think about what we present, but what he can understand and use in what we present.

She outlined the ways in which the organizing principles of young children (aged one to eight) differ from those of adults:

1. Children use language differently from adults. Though they may use the same words adults do, their feelings and understandings about words are different.
   Children are, thus, apt to misinterpret information in advertisements.
2. Children use language less flexibly than adults. After they have described something one way it is difficult for them to describe it in some other way.
   This would account for their tendency to interpret advertising literally. One mother, for example, found her young son cleaning the table with toothpaste. Asked why, he explained: "It worked for me, so it should work for the table."
3. Children cannot think in an orderly, logical fashion since they cannot rehearse their thoughts, or try different solutions or free themselves from their personal interpretations of things. They cannot as easily separate fantasy and reality.
   For this reason, a child would be unable to analyze and judge an ad or to discount its extravagant claims.

4. Even real objects in the world are not constant. A doll without an arm is not the same as a doll with an arm. A sandwich cut on the diagonal is not the same sandwich if it is cut into rectangles.

5. Children look to adults to find out what is "good" and "bad." Experimenters with children report over and over that children are concerned with what adults do and say, even strange adults whom they will never see again.

   Most commercials are delivered by adults, and children are especially susceptible to favorite host characters, whom they trust.

Dr. Rebelsky stated "with certainty" that children's feelings and ideas about TV and commercials are different from those of adults.

Dr. Richard I. Feinbloom, medical director of the Family Health Care Program of Harvard Medical School, wrote a letter, submitted by ACT to the Federal Trade Commission (FTC) for its hearings on the impact of advertising on consumers in November 1971, expressing his concern that all advertising directed at young children is "misleading" because children normally distort reality in accordance with their own immature view of the world:

To children, normally impulsive, advertisements for appealing things demand immediate gratification. An advertisement to a child has the quality of an order, not a suggestion. The child lacks the ability to set priorities, to determine relative importance, and to reject some directives as inappropriate. It is no wonder that children are unable to make a mental correction for the distortion of a piece of merchandise as presented on television, particularly when it is dramatically portrayed with booming voices of announcers, excited child participants, and rousing musical background.

Aaron Locker of Averman, Green & Locker, general counsel to the Toy Manufacturers of America, gave the advertisers' point of view in his statement to the FTC on behalf of the TMA:

Children's attitudes toward commercials are different from the established beliefs of adults. They are more open-minded, more attracted to them. In fact small children have as much interest and warmth for the commercial as for the show.

It seems incredible that anyone should even consider advertising to three-year-olds, knowing how little they understand of what is going on in the world. But it is done all the time on programs that advertisers know attract a large preschool audience.

Research and Advertising

The staff report of the FTC on television advertising to children, released in February 1978, said in summary:

Television commercials are frequently misunderstood by the child audience. Studies show that many children

1. have difficulty in differentiating television commercials from programming;
2. show little understanding that the purpose of commercials is to create product demand; and
3. repose indiscriminate trust in commercial messages, particularly if they are among the group that fails to recognize the selling purpose, or otherwise understand or evaluate, the commercial.

MISLEADING NUTRITION INFORMATION IN ADS

Many people are concerned about the misinformation contained in the ads that children see. For example, many foods advertised to children—snacks, candies, cookies, oversugared cereals—lead to poor nutrition habits. Nutritionists and doctors are particularly concerned about food ads since they know that eating habits formed in childhood are extremely difficult to change. Brand name ads are almost the only food information children receive on TV; they rarely hear of the value of eating vegetables, fresh fruits, cheese, eggs, milk, and orange juice. Instead, glamorized ads for sugar-coated foods, which lead to an excessive craving for sugar, predominate. Ads for toys or other child-oriented merchandise often misrepresent the product by putting it in an idealized context, i.e., in a group of happy friends, a luxurious home situation, or a beautiful outdoor setting.

In March 1973, in testimony before the Senate Select Committee on Nutrition and Human Needs in Washington, D.C., Action for Children's Television stated:

A medium which could be a powerful educational tool to inform the

American public of good health and nutrition is instead a vehicle for falsehood, misinformation, and misleading persuasion. TV advertising presents several dangers to the health of children—the most significant are dental caries, the exclusion of more nutritious foods from the diet, obesity, and other health problems which arise in adulthood as a result of a taste for sweets acquired during childhood.

The consumption of nonnutritious and sugared foods as snacks is a major cause of dental caries. In a study of several hundred five-year-olds, a direct correlation was found between the number of snacks they ate and the number of caries in their teeth. What matters is not the *amount* of sugar ingested but the frequency of intake.[2] An analysis of ads directed to children on a recent Saturday morning found that almost all of the food products were for sweet, sticky snack foods, the most likely to cause caries.

Sugar Strikes A Sour Note

When a leading nutritionist went to the supermarket with some young children, he found himself overwhelmed by the choices in the cereal department.

"As I looked at the array and began to read the lists of ingredients, I became increasingly disturbed by one large question—just how much cereal is in these products?"

Dr. Jean Mayer, president of Tufts University (and former professor of nutrition at the Harvard School of Public Health), knew that product ingredients had to be listed in order of dominance. "Those that read 100 percent whole wheat left little doubt," he noted. "But what about those that read 'whole wheat, sugar, etc.' Were they 97 percent wheat and 2 or 3 percent sugar or 50 percent wheat and 49 percent sugar?"

Dr. Mayer expresses the confusion of many concerned parents who want to give their children nutritious foods but find their children demand sugared cereals with little nutritional value which they have seen advertised on television.

The cereal industry asserts that most cereals contain the same percentage of nutrients, whether they are sugared or not.

"But is this really true?" Mayer asks. "I say no. . . . Whole grain cereals provide protein, calcium, iron, trace minerals, B vitamins, vitamin E in the germ, and fiber in the bran. But some of these nutrients are missing from the high-sugar cereals, which are essentially fortified candy containing other nutrients never found in an ear of corn or grain of wheat. In fact, some of the so-called cereals contain less protein than a candy bar."[3]

How Much Sugar?

At the Veterans Administration Hospital in Houston, Texas, Dr. Ira Shannon and coworkers analyzed 78 ready-to-eat cereals for their sucrose content, since sucrose has been cited as a major factor in the development of tooth decay. Their findings? Twenty-four of the cereals contained 25 to 50 percent sugar and only eight had less than 4 percent. For detailed findings, see Figure 6 below.

SUGARS IN BREAKFAST CEREALS

Sucrose, the proper name for table sugar, a substance made of two simple sugars, glucose and fructose, which must be broken down in the mouth before use. This action makes sucrose the best known fuel for bacteria causing tooth decay.

Glucose, a simple sugar, obtained from food starches, about half as sweet as sucrose and considered less serious as a promoter of tooth decay. It occurs naturally in many fruits and animal tissues and is sometimes known as blood sugar.

Figure 6

Commercial cereal products	Percent sucrose content	Percent glucose content
Shredded Wheat (large)	1.0	0.2
Shredded Wheat (spoon)	1.3	0.3
Cheerios	2.2	0.5
Puffed Rice	2.4	0.4
Uncle Sam Cereal	2.4	1.2
Wheat Chex	2.6	0.9
Grape Nut Flakes	3.3	0.6
Puffed Wheat	3.5	0.7
Alpen	4.1	1.7

Commercial cereal products (cont.)	Percent sucrose content (cont.)	Percent glucose content (cont.)
Post Toasties	4.1	1.7
Product 19	4.1	1.7
Corn Total	4.4	1.4
Special K	4.4	6.4
Wheaties	4.7	4.2
Corn Flakes (Kroger)	5.1	1.5
Peanut Butter	5.2	1.1
Grape Nuts	6.6	1.1
Crispy Rice	7.3	1.5
Corn Chex	7.5	0.9
Corn Flakes (Kellogg)	7.8	6.4
Total	8.1	1.3
Rice Chex	8.5	1.8
Crisp Rice	8.8	2.1
Concentrate	9.9	2.4
Rice Krispies (Kellogg)	10.0	2.9
Raisin Bran (Kellogg)	10.6	14.1
Buck Wheat	13.5	1.5
Granola (dates)	14.5	3.2
Granola (raisins)	14.5	3.8
Sugar Frosted Corn Flakes	15.6	1.8
40% Bran Flakes (Post)	15.8	3.0
Team	15.9	1.1
Brown Sugar-Cinnamon Frosted Mini-Wheats	16.0	0.3
40% Bran Flakes (Kellogg)	16.2	2.1
Granola	16.6	0.6
100% Bran	18.4	0.8
All Bran	20.0	1.6
Granola (almonds)	21.4	1.2
Fortified Oat Flakes	22.2	1.2
Heartland	23.1	3.2
Super Sugar Chex	24.5	0.8
Sugar Frosted Flakes	29.0	1.8
Bran Buds	30.2	2.1
Sugar Sparkled Corn Flakes	32.2	1.8
Frosted Mini Wheats	33.6	0.4
Sugar Pops	37.8	2.9

Commercial cereal products (cont.)	Percent sucrose content (cont.)	Percent glucose content (cont.)
Alpha Bits	40.3	0.6
Sir Grapefellow	40.7	3.1
Super Sugar Crisp	40.7	4.5
Cocoa Puffs	43.0	3.5
Cap'n Crunch	43.8	0.8
Crunch Berries	43.4	1.0
Kaboom	43.8	3.0
Frankenberry	44.0	2.6
Frosted Flakes	44.0	2.9
Count Chocula	44.2	3.7
Orange Quangaroos	44.7	0.6
Quisp	44.9	0.6
Boo Berry	45.7	2.8
Vanilly Crunch	45.8	2.8
Baron von Redberry	45.8	1.5
Cocoa Krispies	45.9	0.8
Trix	46.6	4.1
Froot Loops	47.4	0.5
Honeycomb	48.8	2.8
Pink Panther	49.2	1.3
Cinnamon Crunch	50.3	3.2
Lucky Charms	50.4	7.6
Cocoa Pebbles	53.5	0.6
Apple Jacks	55.0	0.5
Fruity Pebbles	55.1	1.1
King Vitaman	58.5	3.1
Sugar Smacks	61.3	2.4
Super Orange Crisp	68.0	2.8
Mean	**25.1**	**2.3**

Acknowledgment to the *Journal of Dentistry for Children* (September-October 1974), published by the American Society of Dentistry for Children. Reprinted with permission. All rights reserved. For further information, see *Brand Name Guide to Sugar: Sucrose Content of Over 1,000 Common Foods and Beverages* by Ira L. Shannon, D.M.D., M.S.D., Copyright 1977, Nelson-Hall, Chicago.

Sugar Blues

Doctors, dentists, and nutrition educators have become increasingly alarmed at America's high-sugar diet and television's role in promoting it.

Appearing before the United States Select Committee on Nutrition and Human Needs in June 1974, Dr. Abraham Nizel, president of Tufts School of Dental Medicine, said:

Over the last ten years at Tufts, . . . my students and I have done thousands of diet evaluations on patients with rampant [dental] caries. We have never found a single patient whose caries problem could not, in part, be traced to the patient's inordinate consumption of sugar. . . . Sugar-sweetened beverages and hard sucking-type candies such as Lifesavers, cough drops, or breath mints are the worst offenders. Television advertising of these products influences their increased usage.

Dr. Nizel also noted:

Although there is valid concern about the amounts of sugar that are currently used in processed foods, the major consideration is the manner and frequency of ingestion of this sugar. Frequent between-meal snacks of sticky sugar-sweetened confections and foods are the major decay-causing factor. The reasons for this are that the organic acid end products produced by the fermentation of the sugar occurs within seconds and its decalcification effects last for as long as thirty to forty minutes.

If the snack is sticky or sucking type, such as caramels or hard candies, then this acid destruction would continue for perhaps twice the thirty-to-forty minute period before complete buffering of the acid could take place. Thus, snacking sweets at frequent, successive intervals of thirty to forty minutes could conceivably maintain a tooth destroying oral environment on a continuous basis.

Many other professional organizations and experts have expressed their deep concern at the nutritional education the children of America are receiving through television.

In support of ACT's petition to the FTC (April 1977) to promulgate a rule prohibiting TV advertising of candy to children, the Council on Foods and Nutrition, a standing committee of the Board of Trustees of the American Medical Association, commented:

The nature of the advertising and the emphasis on food items of high caloric density (mainly from sugar) that characterize the commercial promotion on children's TV programming is most distressing. There clearly is a need for more responsible advertising that helps to teach the concepts of good health and good nutrition. At the present time, advertising to children is counter productive to the encouragement of sound habits.

The Society for Nutrition Education in California wrote, on the same occasion:

Children are one of the most vulnerable segments of the population, both from the point of view of susceptibility to the advertising message and the physical need for adequate nutrition to ensure their optimal nutritional health for physical and intellectual development. Unfortunately, the nutritional message which is delivered to the child day after day in many TV ads promotes a completely unbalanced diet.

In January 1977, the Select Committee on Nutrition and Human Needs of the United States Senate published its *Dietary Goals for the United States.* These goals recommended the reduction of sugar consumption by about 40 percent to account for about 15 percent of energy intake.

This report too connects sugar with tooth decay—possibly the most widespread disease related to nutrition. In nations of the Far East, where sugar intake per person per year ranged from twelve to thirty-two pounds, the national averages for decayed, missing, or filled teeth in adults twenty to twenty-four years of age ran from 0.9 to 5.

In South American nations, where sugar intake was high (forty-four to eighty-eight pounds per person annually), the averages for decayed, missing, or filled teeth in the same age group ran from 8.4 to 12.6. In the United States today, 98 percent of American children have some tooth decay; by age fifty-five about half of the population of this country have no teeth.

SELLING TOYS TO TOTS

Ever since toy manufacturers discovered television, they have had unique access to our living rooms. Every day the television toy salesman reaches millions of American children with the most impressive techniques the television advertising industry has developed.

No matter how carefully parents explain the logistics of TV advertising to children, few youngsters under twelve can understand that the exciting, fast-moving game shown on the TV screen is not as exciting in real life. Moreover, children are particularly susceptible to the subtle promise that TV-advertised toys bring friends and love.

In a 1975 survey, ACT found that toy commercials accounted for 84 percent of pre-Christmas children's advertising in the afterschool hours on a New York City independent TV station. Moreover, toy commercials made up 47.5 percent of all network children's commercials during the holiday season.

The study, entitled "Pre-Christmas Advertising to Children" and conducted by Dr. F. Earle Barcus of the Boston University School of Public Communications, found that the advertised toys ranged in price from $3.97 to $129.95, with one-half costing more than $12.00. These figures, however, had to be obtained by visiting discount and department stores to price the advertised toys, since none of the ads provided information about what the toys cost.

What's more, product descriptions were inadequate and occasionally misleading. "Although products are visually represented, it is often difficult for the child or adult to determine the materials, physical dimensions, operational procedures, or other necessary consumer information," stated Barcus. "Warnings or cautions about the use of products are seldom given." He found that visual distortion and other special effects were often used; in commercials for the "Six Million Dollar Man" doll, for example, the figures appeared to be walking without human help. "This may lead a child to have unrealistic expectations of product performance," Barcus said.

Another frequently used technique was the promotion of two or more playthings in the same commercial. Barcus notes: "Although you can buy the figures separately, the toy may seem to the child to be incomplete if all the items shown are not purchased."

In response to consumer pressure, toy advertisers provide additional product information by the use of disclaimers. For example, statements such as "partial assembly required," or "all sold separately," or "only in specially marked boxes" may be flashed on the screen and/or included in the commercial's narration. Although these announcements purportedly clarify advertising messages, the vocabulary of most disclaimers is far too advanced for young viewers.

Dr. Robert Liebert, a noted authority on television and children, conducted research to see if children understood disclaimers. He found that the majority of young viewers did not. However, if the wording of the disclaimer was altered to read, for example, "this toy does not come with all its parts—you have to buy them separately," or "you have to put the pieces together yourself," or "only some boxes have these," the children were more likely to comprehend them. Even then, some children were unable to read the message or simply did not understand why the words appeared on the screen.[4]

In addition to its potential to mislead and manipulate young viewers, TV toy advertising has also influenced the kind of products that are being offered to children. ACT's Peggy Charren comments: "Toys are designed to make good thirty-second messages, not to make good toys. That's why you have all these dolls that walk, talk, roll over, and so on. They can each do one thing, which looks great on TV. But you can't even hug the dolls because of all that machinery in their middle."[5]

NOTES

[1] *Who Is Talking to Our Children?* p. 45.
[2] Abraham Nizel, *Nutrition in Preventive Dentistry: Science and Practice* (Philadelphia: 1972), p. 35.
[3] "Cereals or Candy," *Boston Sunday Globe,* November 30, 1975.
[4] Robert Liebert et al., *Effects of Television Commercial Disclaimers on the Product Expectations of Children* (Stony Brook, NY: 1976).
[5] Quoted in Richard Zoglin, "The Coming Battle over TV Ads for Kids," *The New York Times* (January 1, 1978).

The Federal Trade Commission and Children's Advertising

9

The Federal Trade Commission (FTC) is empowered to terminate deceptive advertising campaigns and has, on occasion, acted to protect the public against false or misleading claims, notably those of International Telephone and Telegraph (ITT) in selling Wonderbread, and more recently, claims promoting STP Motor Oil.

ACT AND THE FEDERAL TRADE COMMISSION

ACT's belief that advertising directed at children is essentially unfair led the organization to the FTC as early as 1971 and 1972. ACT filed general petitions with the commission, asking it to prohibit the selling of edibles and toys to children on TV. In 1972 complaints against major drug companies were filed in an attempt to stop the advertising of vitamins directly to children, and in March 1973, ACT filed specific complaints against cereal and candy companies and the CBS TV network for advertising sugared edibles to children. In response to a request from FTC chairman Lewis Engman in 1974, ACT and other consumer representatives worked out a detailed code of proposed guidelines to apply to industries advertising on TV, but broadcasters and advertisers called the compromise unacceptable: they claimed that self-regulation was the answer, that government regulations were not needed.

Spider-Man Squashed?

Despite industry claims, however, self-regulation was not working, and no case better illustrates the need for strong FTC action than that of Spider-Man Vitamins, a product of Hudson Pharmaceutical Corporation.

ACT had achieved a minor victory in 1972 when the National Association of Broadcasters agreed to prohibit the selling of vitamins to children in its *Television Code* (see Chapter 7). Yet only three years later, the misleading and potentially dangerous practice of advertising vitamins to children reappeared.

The Spider-Man Vitamins ads featured a popular and widely recognized comic book character and children's television hero, Spider-Man, as the spokesman for the product (see Figure 7), and were aired during programs for which children constitute up to one-third of the viewing audience. The $1 million campaign to promote these vitamins utilized, according to the marketing director of Hudson, "the most popular personality among children today."

In October 1975, ACT asked the FTC to bring suit to prohibit television commercials promoting Spider-Man Vitamins.

ACT president Peggy Charren explained that "children's chewable vitamins and Spider-Man Vitamins, in particular, are promoted to appear candy-like in form and employ cartoon characters as part of the selling technique, which creates a completely distorted notion of the medicinal contents of the bottle."

Writing in support of the ACT petition, Dr. Richard Feinbloom, medical director of the Family Health Care Program at Harvard Medical School, stated: "The fact is that children, with special exceptions, do not need vitamin supplements. . . . In addition, this particular product (Spider-Man Vitamins) can be criticized because of its potential for accidental iron poisoning, the sugar coating of the tablets which is injurious to teeth, and the implication that the children can expect to achieve superhuman powers when the vitamin is taken."

In September 1976, the FTC agreed with ACT's contentions and issued a consent order prohibiting Hudson Pharmaceutical Corporation from "directing its advertising for Spider-Man and other children's vitamins to child audiences." For the first time, a government regulatory agency recognized that the impact of advertising on children may differ significantly from its impact on adults. In the commission's own words, "Children are unqualified by age or experience to decide for themselves whether or not they need or should use multiple vitamin supplements in general or an advertised brand in particular."

Chasing The Sugar Blues

Armed with the Spider-Man precedent, ACT pursued its battle against TV advertising of highly sugared foods to children. In Peggy Charren's words, "If adults are encouraged to reach for caramel-coated popcorn, it is unfortunate. But it is totally irresponsible to teach children to prefer food products that will be detrimental to their health as they grow."

Televised candy ads which unfairly induce children to eat sugared snacks that cause tooth decay were the subject of ACT's April 1976 petition to the Federal Trade Commission. At the same time, ACT also filed four individual complaints against the Nestle Company, the Fox-Cross Candy Company, the Squibb Corporation, and Mars, Inc.

The organization cited statistics that tooth decay afflicts 98 percent of American children and that $4.7 billion is spent yearly by Americans on dental bills. The petition argued that it is unfair to subject children to glamorous commercials advocating candy consumption when experts agree that most youngsters lack the sophistication necessary to deal with advertising. Studies have shown that children prefer food advertised on television, that they request this food, and that these requests result in parental yielding or family conflict.

The petition stated: "The child may believe the entire commercial message, parrot its words, and remember the name of the product without appreciating the motive of the advertiser. Neither will the child recognize the health problems related to the consumption of these products."

The filing of ACT's petition concerning candy ads coincided with the appointment of Michael Pertschuk as Chairman of the Federal Trade Commission. A long-time supporter of consumer

1. (SFX) MAN: Hi. I'm Spider-Man.

2. My Spider scent tells me that when your children don't eat properly

5. New Super hero vitamins kids won't forget to take.

6. Spider scent reminds them Spider-Man Vitamins

Figure 7

interests, Mr. Pertschuk quickly expressed his concerns about advertising to children. Speaking at ACT's Research Workshop on Televised Role Models and Young Adolescents in November 1977, the chairman commented: "Shouldn't society apply the law's strictures against commercial exploitation of children, and the law's solicitude for the health of children, to ads that threaten to cause imminent harm—harm which ranges from increasing tooth decay and malnutrition to injecting unconscionable stress into the parent-child relationship?"

Cookies For Breakfast? Heavens No!

Although ACT's major FTC petition of 1977 focused on TV

3. they may need
   daily vitamins.

4. So Hudson invented delicious
   chewables, Spider-Man
   Vitamins.

7. has the Parent's Magazine
   seal.

8. For the Hudson Drug Store
   near you, call 800-648-4844.

candy ads, the cereal industry also reached a new low in TV advertising practices.

Ralston Purina introduced a new cereal called "Cookie Crisp," advertising the product to children with 30-second and 60-second TV commercials. (See Figure 8). Noting that such advertising "creates for the child the impression that it is nutritionally desirable to consume cookies for breakfast," ACT filed a complaint with the FTC seeking to ban the commercials. In ACT's words, "It is incredible that a major manufacturer has to resort repeatedly to manipulative tactics directed to children in order to stay in business."

In addition, advertising campaigns for General Food's Cocoa Pebbles and Ralston Purina's Jack-in-the-Box Restaurants were the subjects of ACT legal actions during 1977.

1. VOICE: Hello everybody. And hi.

2. Ho Ho. Here's new Cookie Crisp Cereal you can try.

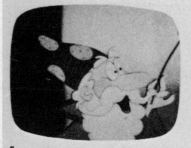

5. I'm Cookie Jarvis with my magic flower

6. to change your dish

9. VOICE: Oh ho. But when you slunk them in milk they stay crisp as could be.

10. Part of a complete breakfast.

Figure 8

3. CHILD: Cookies for breakfast?

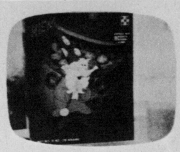

4. VOICE: Heaven's no. Uhless they are my cereal you know.

7. into a cookie jar.

8. CHILD: They look like little cookies to me.

11. I hope you'll favor chocolate chip and vanilla wafer flavor.

12. CHILDREN: Cookie Crisp Cereal.

CHANGING TIMES?

Concern about commercials directed to children is growing, and ACT's long battle to protect young viewers from deceptive TV advertising has led to significant regulatory action during 1978. The interest of the Federal Trade Commission and the support of a wide range of health and professional groups testifies to the issue's significance. In a July 1977 meeting with the FTC, ACT was joined by organizations representing 82,000 teachers and principals, 68,000 health professionals (including 18,000 pediatricians), 11 million parents and other concerned adults, and over 400 agencies serving families and children. Among these organizations were: American Academy of Pediatrics; Dental Health Section of the American Public Health Association; Black Child Development Institute; The Children's Foundation; Child Welfare League of America; East Coast Migrant Head Start Program; Latino Media Task Force; National Association of Elementary School Principals; National Congress of Parent-Teacher Associations; National Council of Negro Women; and the National Women's Political Caucus.

In February 1978, the Federal Trade Commission voted unanimously to open an inquiry into children's TV advertising. The Commission's staff has proposed the following rules to restrict children's commercials:

a *ban* on all television advertising directed at *children under 8* (on the grounds that they are too young to understand the commercial intent of ads)

a *ban* on *television advertising* to *children between ages 8 and 12* of the *highly sugared foods most likely to promote dental decay* (on the grounds that they cannot evaluate the dental risks involved in eating highly sugared foods)

corrective advertising (nutritional disclosures) to balance commercials for *other sugared foods* (on the grounds that children cannot make discriminating choices about diet and nutrition unless they are given more complete information than is presented in current ads)

The public is urged to send opinions concerning these proposed rules to the FTC (see Resource Directory for address).

AND A NOTE:

The Dutch Advertising Council has ruled that ads for sweet foods have no place on the airwaves before 8:00 P.M. The policy effectively eliminates all candy advertising from children's programs.

Young actors under fourteen are prohibited from ever appearing in ads for sweets.

On adult broadcasts, the council has issued an order that will require every candy commercial to devote at least 10 percent of each screen image to an insignia composed of a toothbrush and toothpaste.

The Selling Game and How to Win It

There are different ways of helping children to cope with the pressures of attractive but misleading ads. In an article in *Woman's Day* in November 1972 entitled "Teaching a Child to Think," Fredelle Maynard stated:

Critical thinking is not just the habit of criticizing; it involves the ability to suspend judgement, to examine before accepting, to consider alternatives before making a choice. In developing this art, children need all the help they can get—and they should get it early.

Reasoning and discussion can stimulate an older child to learn how to judge advertising and to make his or her own decisions. But it is unreasonable to expect a preschool child, who is having trouble tying shoelaces, to demonstrate the same capabilities. One conscientious mother watching TV with her five-year-old, carefully explained that the Jumbo Truck being advertised would not really look the same in the store, that it didn't come with all the extra parts being shown, and that it would probably break very easily. The child nodded wisely and even repeated some of her phrases. Then, turning back to the screen, the child said firmly: "I want a Jumbo Truck for my birthday."

Preschool children are just too young to comprehend the intricacies of commercialism on their own programs and too inexperienced to make reasoned consumer judgements, no matter how much information they are given.

Parents can:

Watch commercials with children and try to put the exaggerated claims into perspective. "You know that film is speeded up and no car can really go that fast." Or "Isn't that the toy in the cereal that broke the last time we got it?"

Teach children to write their own commercials and reason out why certain kinds of statements are made.

Analyze the specific appeal of the commercial. "I bet everyone thinks they'll get all those friends if they buy that game, but of course they won't." Or "How can any food make you grow so fast—that's ridiculous."

Take children to the store and compare the ad with the actual product, if you think this will be effective. Some parents feel that this is too tempting and that they will end up buying the product because of pleading from the child, even if they feel it has been misrepresented.

Only watch noncommercial children's television so that young children won't be exposed to commercials.

Ask your doctor or school nurse for a simple poster or chart of nutritional needs for growing children, or design one yourself if you feel creative. In order to counteract food advertisements on television, educate your children about the kinds of foods they need to eat for healthy growth.

Make rules about breakfast cereals—the most common product advertised to children. Some parents refuse to buy any cereal with a premium in the box. Other parents refuse to buy a cereal in which sugar is the first—which means that it is the major—ingredient listed. Other parents, having found that many of the "junk" cereals are bought for premiums or free offers and never get eaten, will only buy a cereal again if it is eaten up the first time.

Encourage children to eat healthy snacks instead of prepackaged cakes and cookies, and have nutritious foods easily available.

Older children might enjoy inventing their own snacks—pizzas on muffins, tomato slices on sticks, peanut butter on crackers—and making their own poster of suggestions. Perhaps you might like to help them get started and then leave them to invent their own.

DANCE A TANGO WITH A MANGO

ACT has developed NUTRITION GAMES/JUEGOS DE NUTRICION, a bilingual poster designed to show Spanish- and English-speaking children that good foods can be as much fun to eat as their TV-advertised counterparts. (See Figure 9.)

In addition to its graphic montage of city life, ACT's bilingual poster includes illustrated ingredients for easy-to-make snacks; hints about how to curtail cavities by stamping out "the sugar sneak"; suggestions for children to contribute their own food designs to the poster; and a crossword puzzle, or "crucigrama" to help young consumers identify tasty and appealing natural foods.

NUTRITION GAMES is supplemented by a set of bilingual educational materials for parents and teachers, designed to "help children keep the nutritious super-snack habit." It contains an assortment of recipes for appetizers and simple meals that children can prepare themselves; instructions for games and tasting parties; and information about the content of TV-advertised foods.

THE TOY PLOYS

ACT has learned that the idea behind toy advertising is to excite the child to bug the parents to buy that particular toy by brand name. The child absorbs the ad's promise that having the toy will make him happy, loved, and surrounded by friends. Parents who recognize the effects of such ads can try to cope in several ways. TV newscaster Barbara Walters has said that she refuses to buy any TV-advertised toys for her child. Other parents teach children that "if a toy's on TV, it can't be any good." These are drastic remedies, and to complicate the issue, a few creative quality toys are advertised on television, usually to parents.

ACT offers you three techniques of defense against the onslaught of toy advertising.

1. The Toy Trap Rap: A Parent-Child Dialogue

Issuing a blanket rule prohibiting any purchases of toys advertised on television puts a tremendous strain on the parent-child relationship. Instead, point out to your children some of the

Figure 9

common-sense reasons why it is impossible to buy everything they see on TV. For example, if all the toys your children want were actually bought, there might not be room to live in your house or apartment.

Use the TV ads for consumer education. List all the toys your child wants, price them, add up the amount, and then translate it into the number of weeks it would take to earn the money, based on weekly allowances.

Price before you promise, since TV-advertised toys are usually very expensive and commercials can be ambiguous about the true contents of a prepackaged toy. For example, the TV ads for the Lone Ranger doll also include Tonto and the bad guy, though each is sold separately. When children ask for one of them they naturally assume that the others are also included.

Suggest creative substitutes for TV toys. Ads for Barbie's Townhouse, which costs about $20, claim that is the "ideal environment" for Barbie. Twenty dollars is a lot of money to pay for a toy, even for affluent parents, and a transformed orange crate or shoe box could be just as appropriate and twice as much fun to make!

Compare fast-paced toy ads with the actual performance of a toy. Does your child expect too much from a toy? Explain that toys which appear to be magical on television end up to be pretty ordinary when they fall apart after ten minutes on the playroom floor.

2. Curious Queries: What To Look For Before Buying a Toy

Is the toy worth the price? Will it hold your child's attention for more than two days? An expensive toy should be made to last and provide long-term enjoyment.

Is your child the right age for the toy? TV ads rarely mention an age range, and most Saturday morning programs are directed to what broadcasters call "the two- to eleven-year-old market."

Does the toy have batteries or complicated mechanical parts?

Are they included, or must you buy them separately?

Is the toy safe? Be wary of toys that require electricity or toys that shoot objects in the air, have sharp edges or unfinished surfaces. Small children try putting things into their mouths, so be careful of loose parts. Think of ways that a child could misuse the toy.

3. Self-Defense Techniques: You Can Fight Back

Complain in writing to a manufacturer if you are dissatisfied with his product. Write even if you did *not* buy his product, and tell him why. His name and address will be on the box.

Buy carefully; your purchases speak clearly to the manufacturer. If you buy, he assumes that he has made what you want. Look for a store with a wide selection of toys, and choose the one you can afford.

Tell advertisers, TV stations, and networks about toy commercials that you think are unfair or misleading. Send a copy of your letter to ACT.

Write to the Federal Trade Commission about deceptive toy ads (6th and Pennsylvania Avenues N.W., Washington, D.C. 20580).

Did you know that many experts believe that children do not need the complex, mechanical kinds of toys advertised on television? Dr. James L. Hymes, Jr., professor of education and chairman of the Early Childhood Education Department of the University of Maryland, writes in his book, *The Child Under Six*:[1]

The essence of children's play is that the youngsters build their own meanings and ideas into whatever is at hand. The children themselves are the "toy manufacturers." You don't really have to spend much cash for finished products which have the details worked out.

Indeed, one toy executive admitted that when boxes of new toys are tested on a group of children, the children end up playing games with the empty boxes and ignoring the complicated toys! Television toy ads do not encourage the use of imaginative

"FORTUNATELY . . . . OUR PROSPECTIVE CUSTOMER IS STILL TOO YOUNG AND IRRESPONSIBLE TO FULLY UNDERSTAND THE REAL MEANING OF CHRISTMAS"

Reprinted courtesy of the Boston Globe and Paul Szep.

play and, indeed, television toys may be detrimental to the creative use of simple playthings.

So don't feel guilty about saying no to a TV toy that you don't think is going to be a good present. You have right on your side from the highest places!

QUESTIONS PARENTS ASK

Question: When I was a kid there were ads on radio, and they didn't hurt me. Sure, I wrote off for things and found out if they worked or not. Isn't being exposed to ads part of a child's education?

Answer: Yes—and no. Radio never, never had the amount of advertising directed to children that a child experiences from television today. Even television has never before had so many commercials. In fact, when television began, children's TV shows were aired without commercials as a matter of course. But since the 1960s, the advertising scene has changed so that children are treated as a consumer market, just as adults are.

Consumer-education-by-experience is certainly one way to learn, but it is doubtful whether preschoolers who ordered products advertised on a preschool program and found that they didn't perform as expected would have the mental ability to understand what had really happened. Dr. John Condry, professor of Human Development and Psychology at Cornell University, believes that young children blame themselves when products don't perform as depicted on television, since they are unable to understand that the advertiser was trying to put his product in the best light. Children don't comprehend the complexities behind television commercials.

Broadcasters who care about consumer education for children could produce informative messages for children's programs and save their product ads for adults. But as Cleo Hovel, of the Leo Burnett Ad Agency, said: "Our primary goal is to sell products to children, not educate them."[2]

Question: Don't you think worry about advertising to children is exaggerated? Surely most advertisers don't really mean to take advantage of young children!

Answer: Sadly, many do. In countless meetings with advertisers and by reading trade magazines such as *Advertising Age* and *Television and Radio Age,* we have learned that advertisers consider children only as "a market" and plan campaigns to reach the "two- to eleven-year-old market." One advertising executive said in *Advertising Age* (July 19, 1965):

When you sell a woman on a product and she goes into the store and finds your brand isn't in stock, she'll probably forget about it. But when you sell a kid on your product, if he can't get it, he will throw himself on the floor, stamp his feet and cry. You can't get a reaction like that out of an adult.

Eugene S. Mahany of Needham, Harper and Steers Advertising Agency, wrote in *Broadcasting* magazine (June 30, 1969):

We can shape our future marketing programs on what appeals directly to the child, not to the parent, because if the parent initiates interest, then the appeal is lessened, and the job of selling is made more difficult.

Broadcasters also recognize the potential economic value of the child market. The August 29, 1977, issue of *Broadcasting* contained an advertisement directed to potential television advertisers. The ad proclaimed:

If you're selling, Charlie's Mom is buying. But you've got to sell Charlie first. His allowance is only 50¢ a week, but his buying power is an American phenomenon. He's not only tight with his Mom, but he has a way with his Dad, his Grandma and Aunt Harriet, too.

When Charlie sees something he likes, he usually gets it. Just ask General Mills (or) McDonald's. . . .

Of course, if you want to sell Charlie, you have to catch him when he's sitting down. Or at least standing still. And that's not easy. Lucky for you, Charlie's into TV.[3]

Certainly there are some responsible advertisers for child-oriented products. Fisher-Price, for example, advertises its line of preschool toys only to parents. But most manufacturers will listen to any advertising suggestion that will sell products, even if that means selling to children.

NOTES

[1] Englewood Cliffs, N.J.: 1961, p. 193.

[2] *Advertising Age*, July 19, 1965.

[3] *Staff Report of the Federal Trade Commission on Television Advertising to Children*, February, 1978, p. 98.

Children's Workbook

Television is like potatoes. You can fry them or bake them or boil them or peel them or make french fries or mash them. But they are still potatoes. If you're watching a series on TV, no matter what they do to it, you know that it's going to end happily because it has to go on the next day and that nothing's ever really going to happen, no matter what it is, because it's television. *—David, Age Twelve*

CHILDREN'S WORKBOOK

How much TV do you watch? What do you do the rest of the time? Which programs do you like? The next few pages have several charts for you to complete which will help you to answer those questions.

Diary and Key to Activities

This is to be completed for one full week—or several days. Keep it handy and check how many squares are filled in with TV watching as compared to your other activities (pp. 130–131).

TV Testing Chart

This chart is for you to make notes on what programs you watch and why. Keep it near the television set with a pencil and check it off as you watch (pp. 132–133).

Program Rating Chart

Now you can be a critic. Choose some specific programs you watch, and write down your criticisms and ratings for them. You can do this with any program and grade it in any way you want (pp. 134–135).

DIARY

	MON.	TUES.	WED.
7–8 A.M.			
8–9 A.M.			
9–10 A.M.			
10–11 A.M.			
11–12 A.M.			
12–1 P.M.			
1–2 P.M.			
2–3 P.M.			
3–4 P.M.			
4–5 P.M.			
5–6 P.M.			
6–7 P.M.			
7–8 P.M.			

SUGGESTED KEY

	Watched TV	▭	Read	☼	Played outside
abc	School	🛏	Slept	🚶	Went to friends

DIARY

THURS.	FRI.	SAT.	SUN.

Ate

 Did homework

 Went out with parents

Played with brother/sister

Played alone inside

Design other symbols for your other activities.

YOUR TV TESTING CHART

	MON.	TUES.	WED.
Date			
Program Title and Time on			
Who chose and Why			
Program Title and Time on			
Who chose and Why			
Program Title and Time on			
Who Chose and Why			
Program Title and Time on			
Who Chose and Why			

Put this near your TV set and fill it in.

YOUR TV TESTING CHART

THURS.	FRI.	SAT.	SUN.

PROGRAM RATING CHART

Name of program and station or network it is on	Length of program and number of commercials	Description of program

PROGRAM RATING CHART

9 8 7 Good	6 5 4 OK	3 2 1 Poor	Comments

EXPERIMENTS FOR YOUR TV VIEWING

Experiment 1: The Turn-Off

Try setting aside a definite period of time for not watching TV at all. It might be a few days, a full week, a weekend. But make

1. EXPERIMENT: THE TURN-OFF

	MON.	TUES.	WED.
7–8 A.M.			
8–9 A.M.			
9–10 A.M.			
10–11 A.M.			
11–12 A.M.			
12–1 P.M.			
1–2 P.M.			
2–3 P.M.			
3–4 P.M.			
4–5 P.M.			
5–6 P.M.			
6–7 P.M.			
7–8 P.M.			

What did you do when you turned off TV? (You can use the Key to Activities from the Diary)

it a definite time, and keep a careful diary of what you do instead of watching TV. You can then compare that with your chart for viewing times. Maybe you could ask your parents or grandparents what they did when they didn't have television.

THE TURN-OFF

THURS.	FRI.	SAT.	SUN.

Experiment 2: My Perfect Viewing Room

Imagine you could design your own Video Space which would be the ideal place for watching television. What would it look like? What would it need? Where should it be? Why would it be perfect? Write a description of your perfect viewing room or draw it.

Experiment 3: Design Your Own Program

You've probably seen dozens of television programs. What do you remember about them? What did you like or dislike? How were they put together?

Imagine that someone gave you half an hour of TV time to produce your own program. What would you put into those minutes—news, discussion, puppets, movies, sports? Plan it out—it's all yours. (Begin here and then use as many sheets of paper as you need.)

TV show title: . . . .   Length: . . . .

Producer: . . . .   Staff: . . . .

Opening shot: . . . .

For a TV script you write the action in one column and the dialogue in another:

Shot of cowboy on horse.

Pan to horizon and clouds.

JEFF: Where did you last see the wild stallion?

MIKE: Out there to the west.

CONSUMERISM

An eleven-year-old girl named Dawn Ann Kurth from Melbourne, Florida, became interested in advertising to children because of her younger sister:

"My sister Martha, who is seven, had asked my mother to buy a box of Post Raisin Bran so that she could get the free record that was on the back of the box. It had been advertised several times on Saturday morning cartoon shows. My mother bought the cereal, and we all (there are four children in our family) helped Martha eat it so she could get the record.

"It was after the cereal was eaten and she had the record that the crisis occurred. There was no way the record would work.

"Martha was very upset and began crying and I was angry too. It just didn't seem right to me that something could be shown on TV that worked fine and people were listening and dancing to the record and when you bought the cereal, instead of laughing and dancing, we were crying and angry."

Dawn had been chosen with thirty-five other students at Meadowlane Elementary School to do a project in any field they wanted. She decided to find out how other children felt about deceptive advertising. She began by watching television one Saturday morning, and clocked twenty-five commercial messages during one hour, 8:00 to 9:00, not counting ads for shows coming up or public service announcements. She also discovered that during shows her parents liked to watch there were only ten to twelve commercials each hour, which surprised her.

Dawn devised a questionnaire and asked 1,538 children the following questions:

Quiz

1. Do you ask your mother to buy products you see advertised on TV? Yes   No
2. Did you ever buy a product to get the free bonus gift inside? Yes   No
3. Were you satisfied? Yes   No
4. Write down an example.
5. Do you believe that certain products you see advertised on TV make you happier or have more friends? Yes   No

6. Please write an example.
7. Did you ever feel out of it because your mother wouldn't buy a certain product? Yes   No
8. Did you ever feel your mother was mean because she wouldn't buy the product you wanted? Yes   No

Answer these questions yourself.*

Some adults concerned with advertising to children heard about Dawn's study, and Senator Frank E. Moss invited her to appear before the Senate Subcommittee for Consumers at special hearings on May 31, 1972. Dawn's testimony explained her concerns and outlined the survey she had carried out. Her testimony is now part of the Senate record of hearings.

For You to Do: Do Your Own Think!

What do you think about advertising to children?

Can you think of ways to help young children understand about ads on television?

Does anything bother you about some of the ads you may see?

What do you like about ads on television?

If there have to be ads on television, how many would be the ideal number for you in one hour?

Write down your answers on a sheet of paper.

DO-IT-YOURSELF
Your Own Cartoon

You must have seen plenty of TV cartoons. Did you know that each cartoon is made up of hundreds and hundreds of drawings, which are then filmed?

On the next two pages are a series of squares for you to design your own cartoon story. It can be anything at all. It can look like anything at all. It's all yours! (You can turn the book sideways if you want.)

---

*Dawn got the following responses to her questionnaire: 1) Yes, 203; No 330. 2) Yes 1,120; No 413. 3) Yes 668; No 873. 5) Yes 1,113; No 420. 7) Yes 802; No 735. 8) Yes 918; No 620.

THIS CARTOON IS CALLED:

YOUR OWN PUBLIC SERVICE ANNOUNCEMENT (PSA)

When advertisers make a commercial or public service announcement they prepare a story board, with drawings of how they think the finished commercial will look. Later it is possible to show what the PSA (see Figure 10) looked like on television by using photos from the film with the words underneath.

Look at this example, and then fill out the blank story board on pp. 146–147 with your own public service announcement. (You can turn the book sideways if you want.)

Figure 10

"I got dibs on the swing!"

"I got here first!" "No, you didn't!"

(VO) What would you do?

"Hey, let's take turns."

(VO) There are lots of things you can do when two people want the same thing.

(VO) One is to take turns!

ID: United Methodists
Disciples of Christ

Produced by United Methodist Communications in cooperation with Media Action Research Center. Reprinted with permission.

THIS PSA IS FOR:

What You Can Do

Perhaps you have read this far and feel that broader action needs to be taken in the sensitive area of children's television programming. Perhaps you are personally involved with children through education or medicine or as a parent. You've come to your own family decisions about how much television to watch and, as best you can, are helping your own children to cope with programming and ads. You feel that since you are meeting your responsibility, you would like to put some pressure on the broadcaster to meet his responsibility to put on more and better programs. Children's television will always be a joint responsibility—shared between the parents, with their natural concern for their own children, and the broadcaster, with his sometimes less apparent concern for the needs of the children in the community he is serving.

A. ALWAYS WRITE

One of the most effective ways to make your voice heard in these days of instant communication is the good, old-fashioned letter. If you see something on television that you like very much, or that bothers you for some reason or other, or that you feel is unsuitable for children, compose a sensible and thoughtful letter, clearly stating your feelings. Type it if you possibly can; handwritten letters don't get the same kind of attention in executive offices as typed letters do. Make some carbon copies and send them out too—as many as you like. And type the names of the people you're sending them to at the bottom of your letter.

For example, you could write a letter to a *local station*, expressing your feelings about the cartoons they are running. In that case, send a copy to the Federal Communications Commission in Washington, D.C. (which keeps a file on every licensed station), and to the network with which the station is affiliated. When the FCC receives a "complaint," it usually asks the station to respond, and, very rarely, investigates it. The FCC has the power, however, to levy a fine or issue an order demanding that the station remedy the complaint. In a complaint, state your name, the station's call letters, and your precise complaint or suggestion. If possible, relate this to an FCC standard. Ask for a specific remedy.

You might write a letter to the *sponsor*. Let the sponsor or advertisers know how you feel about programs on which their product ads appear, or about advertising directed to children, or about the performance of the product. You should send a copy of letters like this to the station (or the network) that aired the ad, the FCC, and the Federal Trade Commission in Washington, D.C.

You could write directly to the *network* that originated the program, send a copy to the local station that aired it, and to the FCC and the sponsor.

You might send letters to the *Federal Communications Commission*. The FCC licenses every TV and radio station for three years and is responsible for ensuring that stations meet "the public interest, convenience and necessity" standards. Part of the station's responsibility is to meet the needs of the large child audience which most of them are reaching. The 100,000 letters, filings, and comments that the FCC received during its inquiry into children's television were a persuasive factor in encouraging it to continue the examination of this area.

You might cite specific abuses in advertising to the *Federal Trade Commission*. The FTC is responsible for eliminating unfair or misleading advertising and can accept complaints relating to particular ads.

You could write to the *Food and Drug Administration* in Rockville, Maryland, about food advertising or about specific edible products that are advertised to children on TV. The FDA is also concerned with the sale of dangerous toys.

As a citizen, you can write to *your representative in Congress* and let him or her know your concerns about children's television and advertising. It is always helpful to inform your representative about issues such as this so that he or she will know where the constituency stands on such matters.

And try sending letters to *the press.* Your local TV critic is probably well aware of what is going on in children's TV and would be glad to hear from you. The editor of a weekly paper might be glad to discuss this issue with a local resident and to air it in the pages of the paper.

And Don't Forget The Praise!

It is often easy to type a letter of indignation when the movie about the Boston Strangler is aired at 7:00 P.M. and scares the wits out of your children, who watch some of it before you can turn it off. But don't forget to write the letter complimenting a station that airs a good children's program at a reasonable hour or a station that is making efforts to cluster commercials at the beginnings and ends of children's programs. And send copies of the letters of praise as well as of the letters of complaint to agencies or companies. That's only fair! Most station managers are sensitive to letters from the public.

Never Underestimate the Power of a Letter

If it is a good letter, based on clearly stated facts, chances are that the message will get through to the right place. Don't be afraid to call up and follow through on it if you don't get a reply; that will make doubly sure that your letter isn't ignored.

Useful Addresses

In the Resource Directory there is a list of useful addresses of people to whom you may want to write. You can look up the addresses of your local TV stations in the phone book under their call letters (WNAC-TV, KTVU-TV, etc.) if you need to write to them.

B. BE INFORMED

It is important, when dealing with any controversial issue, to make sure that you have done your homework and know as much as you possibly can about your subject. This is essential in an area as emotionally charged as children's television and the profits from advertising to children. It is not difficult to get the facts, but make sure that you do.

Watch television. That sounds obvious, but it is surprising how many people—while alleging that there is nothing wrong—really have not sat down and looked at any television programs. Choose a specific program or time period. Find a clock with a second hand, some paper and a pencil, and while you watch, take notes on whatever aspect of the program you might be interested in. A recent study of minorities in children's programming was based on careful viewing, for fourteen and a half hours, of Saturday children's programs in which every incident, character, and advertisement was noted down and later analyzed.

Monitoring

In most cases, the most constructive method is to set up a carefully planned monitoring schedule for one specific program or one specific time period. You might design a simple form for monitoring programs with columns for the time of the program, description, and comments. For reference, you should always note the date, station, title of the program, and the name of its producer, which usually appears at the end of the program. When monitoring, it is important to have a clock with a second hand since you may want to note the time and length of ads, announcements, promos, station identification, and introductions and closings of programs. In one half-hour, you may have twenty different items to note, as well as the content of the program segments.

Take notes on whatever aspect of the programming you're interested in. You might decide to time and note the content of ads. Or write down a detailed description of the content of an hour's programming. You might prefer to watch a weekly series over a period of time or a daily series over a period of weeks. It is important to watch a program more than once. Series change week by week and while one story line may be offensive, the next week's program may be quite different.

Instructions For Monitoring

1. You will need: monitoring form (some samples follow)
   two pencils or pens
   clock or watch with a second hand
   to take telephone off the hook
   to tune television in before program begins.

2. Time the show from the beginning through the network break to the start of the next show.

3. Time the commericals accurately in minutes and seconds. Use a clock or stopwatch with an easily visible second hand. The commercials are usually thirty to sixty seconds long. There is no need to time the shows themselves.

4. For each ad, record the sponsor, product, and the length of the message. Add the total time and record in given space.

5. Give a brief synopsis of the story, stories, or other action in the program.

6. Use the back of the form for any additional comments.

7. Make a note of any period when you stop monitoring during the program.

MONITORING FORM FOR CHILDREN'S TELEVISION

Title: _____

Time: _____

Date: _____

Type of Program:

_____ Cartoon   _____ Adult situation comedy

_____ Live action children's   _____ Adult adventure program
       program

	YES	NO
1. Was the program produced during the last two years?	___	___
2. Are the characters from a variety of cultural and ethnic groups?	___	___
3. Is violence shown as a solution to a problem?	___	___
4. Is violence shown as hurting people?	___	___
5. Do the characters care about each other?	___	___
6. Are women shown in a variety of roles?	___	___
7. Is the program specifically designed for a specific age group?	___	___

_____ Under six years _____ Six to ten years _____ ten to fifteen
      years

Comments:

MONITORING FORM FOR CHILDREN'S COMMERCIAL

Program: _____

Time: _____

Date: _____

Product: _____

Manufacturer: _____

Toys

_____ Showed how to operate toy

_____ Showed parts/products not sold with toy

_____ Stressed fun with friends

Photography made toy look:

_____ Larger

_____ Faster

_____ Sounds in commercial cannot be made by toy

_____ Verbal disclaimer

_____ Visual disclaimer

Food

Type:

_____ Breakfast food

_____ Candy

_____ Soft drink

_____ Fast food

_____ Other kinds of food (dairy, vegetable, etc.)

Description:

_____ Made nutritional claims

_____ Stressed sweetness of food

_____ Stressed food as fun

_____ Offered a premium

Comments:

Watching television with your child is the only way to apply what you have read in this book. Otherwise you will know no more about children's television than you would know about a painting from the artist's verbal description.

It is also absolutely essential, when you write letters or make any criticisms of children's television, that you be talking from your own viewing experience. No criticism loses its validity more quickly than one in which the complainant admits: "Well, I didn't actually see the program but. . . ."

In order to keep informed about children's TV, read books and current magazines. Many newspapers have a daily TV column which is worth reading. The Resource Directory includes a bibliography on children's television.

Figure 11 is a professional monitoring summary, showing children's television between 8:00 and 9:30 A.M. one Saturday on Channel 5 (WHDH-TV) in Boston. The symbols (PM,CA, NCA) refer to the segment timed (i.e., program material, commercial announcement, noncommercial announcement). This summary was prepared by Dr. F. Earle Barcus of Boston University as part of his study, *Saturday Children's Television*. Dr. Barcus timed seconds as percentages of a minute.

Figure 11. Monitoring summary, prepared by Dr. F. Earle Barcus

JUNE 19, 1971, 8:00 A.M. to 9:30 A.M.

Bugs Bunny/Roadrunner Hour

			Minutes
8:00:00	PM	"Bugs Bunny/Roadrunner Hour" (Intro.)	1.75
8:01:45	CA	(Kool Aid)	.50
8:02:15	CA	(Kool Pop)	.50
8:02:45	PM	"Bunker Hill Bunny" (Cartoon)	6.67
8:09:25	CA	(Romper Room's Inchworm Toy)	.50
8:09:55	CA	(Grape Tang)	.50
8:10:25	PM	(Roadrunner Song and Chase) (Transition)	.42
8:10:50	CA	(General Mills' Count Chocula Cereal)	.50
8:11:20	CA	(General Mills' Cheerios)	.50
8:11:50	PM	"Tweety's Circus" (Cartoon)	6.57
8:18:25	CA	(Keebler's Cookies)	.50
8:18:55	CA	(Keebler's Cookies)	.50
8:19:25	PM	"Bugs Bunny/Roadrunner Hour" (Transition)	.42
8:19:50	CA	(Mattel's Dawn Doll)	.50
8:20:20	CA	(Mattel's Zoomer Boomer)	.50
8:20:50	PM	"Gee Whizz" (Cartoon)	5.83
8:26:40	CA	(Post Sugar Crisp)	.50
8:27:10	CA	(Kool Pop)	.50
8:27:40	PM	"Stay tuned for part two" (Transition)	.42
8:28:05	NCA	"Keep Boston Clean"	.17
8:28:15	CA	(Birdseye Libbyland Frozen Dinners)	1.00
8:29:15	ID	"WHDH-TV" (VO): "Lassie" as visual	.08
8:29:20	PM	"Bugs Bunny/Roadrunner Hour" (Transitional)	.50
8:29:50	CA	(Kellogg's Raisin Bran)	.50
8:30:20	PM	"Hare Ways to the Stars" (Cartoon)	6.25
8:36:35	CA	(Nestles Quik)	.50
8:37:05	CA	(Nestles $100,000 Bar)	.50
8:37:35	PM	"Bugs Bunny/Roadrunner Hour" (Transitional)	.50
8:38:05	CA	(General Mills' Cheerios)	.50
8:38:35	CA	(Kenner's SST Racer)	.50
8:39:05	PM	"Highway Runnery" (Cartoon)	6.00
8:45:05	CA	(Hershey Bars)	.50
8:45:35	CA	(Old Spice for Father's Day)	.50
8:46:05	PM	"Bugs Bunny/Roadrunner Hour" (Transitional)	.50
8:46:35	CA	(General Mills' Count Chocula/Frankenberry)	1.00
8:47:35	PM	"Bonanza Bunny" (Cartoon)	5.84
8:53:25	CA	(Quaker Cereals—Willy Wonka premium)	1.00
8:54:25	Promo	"Groovie Ghoulies and Sabrina"	.33
8:54:45	PM	"Bugs Bunny/Roadrunner Hour" (Visuals, Credits)	1.08
8:55:50	NCA	(Seat Belts)	.33

In the Know

8:56:10	PM	"In the Know"—"by Kellogg's"	.33
8:56:30	CA	(Kellogg's Rice Krispies)	.50
8:57:00	PM	"In the Know"—"Saturday in Rome"	1.68
8:58:40	Promo	(Captain Kangaroo) (CBS)	.33
8:59:00	CA	(McDonald's)	.50
8:59:30	NCA	(Boys' Club of America)	.50

Figure 11. Monitoring summary (cont.)

The Groovie Ghoulies and Sabrina the Teenage Witch

9:00:00	ID	"WHDH-TV Boston" (Identification)	.08
9:00:05	PM	"Groovie Ghoulies . . ." (Jokes à la Laugh-In)	2.42
9:02:30	PM	"Hansel and Gretel" (Cartoon)	2.67
9:05:10	PM	"Horrible Horrorscope" (Cartoon)	2.08
9:07:15	CA	(General Mills' Count Chocula Cereal)	.50
9:07:45	CA	(Tang)	.50
9:08:15	PM	"Don't go away" (Transition)	.50
9:08:45	CA	(Romper Room's Inchworm Toy)	.50
9:09:15	CA	(General Mills' Count Chocula/Frankenberry)	.50
9:09:45	PM	"Beach Party" (Cartoon)	3.58
9:13:20	CA	(Pillsbury's Funny Face)	.50
9:13:50	CA	((Stuckey's—"Happy Highways" premium)	.50
9:14:20	PM	"Stick around" (Transition)	.33
9:14:40	CA	(Kellogg's Special K)	.50
9:15:10	CA	(Kellogg's Frosted Mini-Wheat)	.50
9:15:40	PM	"Beach Party" (Continued)	5.42
9:21:05	PM	"Don't go away" (Transition)	.33
9:21:25	CA	(Mattel's Dawn Doll and Friends)	.50
9:21:55	CA	(Shasta Soda)	.25
9:22:10	CA	(Burger King)	.50
9:22:40	PM	"Noises are the Strangest Things in the World" (Song)	2.67
9:25:20	CA	(Quaker Cereals—Willy Wonka premium)	1.00
9:26:20	PM	"Don't go away" (Transition)	.58
9:26:55	Promo	"The Week Ends Here"	.25
9:27:10	CA	(Spokies)	.50
9:27:40	CA	(McDonalds)	.50
9:28:10	ID	"WHDH-TV Boston" (Visual Red Sox)	.09
9:28:15	PM	"Stick around" (Transition)	.42
9:28:40	CA	(Sizzler's Fat Track)	.50
9:29:15	PM	"Weird Window Time" (Jokes à la Laugh-In)	3.34

C. COOPERATION

If you want to bring about real change, it is difficult to do it alone. If you can get together with a few friends, a local group, or an organization, you stand a much better chance of making waves and bringing about valid changes. That is how Action for Children's Television began.

Now an established international organization, ACT began one cold New England winter night when Peggy Charren invited concerned parents, educators, and friends to her house to sit in the living room and discuss television and violence and their effects on children.

From that first meeting others followed, and eventually a core group of four women—Peggy Charren, Lillian Ambrosino, Judith Chalfen, and Evelyn Kaye Sarson—became the first working staff of Action for Children's Television in 1968. ACT has changed since those meetings with neighborhood friends in Peggy Charren's living room. ACT is now an organization with a paid staff of ten, including a full-time attorney, and has over one hundred volunteer representatives and fifteen affiliated groups across the country and in other countries. In 1970, money for long-distance phone calls and trips to New York and Washington came from household savings. Today ACT's $300,000 budget is met by dues from more than 10,000 members and by grants from foundations and corporations.

Local Contacts and Committees

Over one hundred active members make up Action for Children's Television's national network of contacts. Serving as liaisons between ACT and local communities, these concerned citizens act as resource persons in children's television, distribute ACT information, display ACT materials, speak to local organizations and groups, appear on radio and TV, talk to local broadcasters, and work to educate community leaders and members about children and television. Several dedicated contacts have been instrumental in the formation of local children's television committees.

ACT has never set up any chapters but encourages local groups to form their own committees as independent units to deal with local problems in children's television. ACT provides assistance and information but in no way dictates policy or direction to local groups. Perhaps you might like to set up a committee in your area or find out if one is already being set up. (See Resource Directory for list of cities with ACT contacts.)

Every area has different television, depending upon the caliber of its program managers and station owners. For example, Boston has very different programming today from what it had ten years ago. One reason is that the local noncommercial public TV station has become a strong and popular force in the community, with a devoted viewing audience. The second is that, in an unprecedented license challenge case, the license of a VHF station was given to a new group of owners, who have made great efforts to upgrade local programming. And the third reason is the presence in the Boston community of citizen groups, including ACT, concerned about programming.

The best thing a local group can do is to provide a sounding board for community ideas and interests and to be a source of information. At a preliminary meeting, for example, an open discussion of what is good or bad about local television might pinpoint some specific issues: no children's programs in the late afternoon, no programs for a large minority group within the community, an excessive number of reruns of old violent programs or other similar problems. Or the interest of the group might lead it to examine one specific area, for example, programming for Spanish-speaking viewers or for the deaf. The group could then decide on the kind of action it would like to be involved in, beginning, perhaps, with letters to the stations, meetings with local program managers, articles in local newspapers, and discussions with other interested community leaders.

Local committees on children's television can have far-reaching impact on the broadcasting situation in their area. Few broadcasters have any real knowledge of children, of child development, or of how television affects children. They respond to community comment. If a responsible local group can show local broadcasters that it is to their advantage, as well as to the benefit of the child audience, to program the best and most interesting programs that they can find, then they will be more inclined to do so. It is essential for them to know that if they do make an effort, the attempts will be noticed and commented upon. Don't complain bitterly about a program of poor quality being offered to children in your community and then forget to thank the broadcasters when they replace it with an excellent series of children's films. Local groups and contacts may have their greatest success in the area of community education. Some of the ways committees have educated parents, health professionals, educators, broadcasters, and community leaders about children and television include:

Setting up a speakers bureau

Publishing a newsletter

Creating informative brochures and booklets

Designing slide shows

Appearing on radio and television, writing articles for newspapers, magazines, and journals

Organizing conferences and workshops

Conducting monitoring studies, developing viewing guidelines

Writing school curricula

Teaching college courses

Sponsoring children's activities festivals

Producing local public service announcements

D. WHAT EFFECTS CAN PRESSURE HAVE?

Pressure and public comment can certainly have an effect on some aspects of children's television. Some broadcasters will ignore all criticisms and suggestions, but often others are ready to discuss problems and listen to ideas for improvement. Most efforts for change, however, take time and dedication.

In Boston, in September 1969, the local CBS outlet cut off the network program "Captain Kangaroo" halfway through the show. "Captain Kangaroo" was the only children's program available at that hour in Boston, and many parents called ACT to suggest that something be done. Several courses of action were taken:

1. Letters were written to the station by ACT, and other parents were urged to write to the station and local newspapers.

2. Two ACT members met with the general manager of the TV station and his assistant. The broadcasters explained that the expansion of their morning news show necessitated cutting the "Captain Kangaroo" hour. ACT was not convinced; the station ran several other news programs but did not have a single minute of children's programming at other times of the day.

3. ACT organized a "Good-Natured Picket for Good Television" outside the station, with placards reading "Captain Kangaroo —All of You."

4. The station sent out a two-page letter to all who wrote in, explaining the cut. This backfired, since many parents were furious at the longwinded explanations and urged their friends and relatives to write, protesting the cut.

In January 1970, after thirteen weeks, the station reinstated the full hour of "Captain Kangaroo." ACT's efforts were credited with the restoration of the program.

Any attempt to bring about a change in children's television must:

have a clearly focused objective which is limited in scope

be planned carefully, so that you know what to expect

be reasonable in demanding changes

be properly researched and backed up with indisputable facts

be legal

be representative of the community, not just one individual

What Some Groups Have Done

Local committees on children's television are formed to represent the citizens in their communities. Most groups work within a single broadcasting market, for example, in Atlanta, Detroit, Seattle, and Lancaster (PA). Other groups, such as the New York Council on Children's Television and the Colorado Committee on Children's Television, are expanding their concerns and are becoming statewide. Either way, broadbased support is essential to an effective local committee.

In addition, the California Committee on Children's Television (CCT), based in San Francisco, now has an active group in Los Angeles. Because the California committee is the oldest and most established of the local groups, it has been involved in some exciting and far-reaching activities. CCT has filed a one-billion-dollar class-action suit in Los Angeles Superior Court against General Foods' Post Cereals Division for "using a high-pressure multi-media campaign which exploits trusting children in order to sell sugar concoctions as nutritious breakfast cereals." The California committee has also cooperated with other California consumer groups to file a multi-million-dollar class-action suit against Mattel, Inc. The groups charged that the toy company's television advertisements directed to young children are phony and misleading. An ethnically diverse board of advisors, a permanent staff, and many volunteers have enabled CCT to become a visible force for upgrading children's television within the community.

E. SUGGESTIONS FOR FORMING A GROUP

If you would like to try cooperating with some other people, it is often best to set up an informal meeting, at which you might show a film or watch some television programs for children, or perhaps watch videotapes of children's television programs and commercials. Then encourage a general discussion and see what happens. The meeting might decide to set up a committee, with a chairman, treasurer, and director, and with a definite plan of action and future meetings. Or it might simply have a philosophical talk about what television is doing to children and what it could be doing. Or it might be a place for parents to air their gripes about local programs, or discuss how they cope with TV watching in their homes. Or it could be a good place to publicize programs worth looking out for or programs to avoid.

Try to leave the meeting reasonably open, unless there is some clear local issue that urgently needs attention, and examine the mood of the participants. In some areas, the cancellation of a popular program may bring out a highly motivated group of viewers determined to work for its return. This can be an excellent basis for beginning a constructive group effort.

In many cases, the most constructive way is to set up a carefully scheduled monitoring program for one specific program or one specific time period, with two people watching each program daily, or weekly, over a short period of time. This can provide invaluable raw material for further action and discussion.

Whatever you do to encourage interest within your community is really "consciousness-raising" for those who participate, since it will increase their awareness of how much influence television does have in the lives of our children.

Planning a Meeting

If you are interested in planning a meeting about children and television, the following suggestions may be helpful in making your decisions. A program about children and television should cover the following topics:

the amount of television watched

the effects of television on children

what children learn from watching television

suggestions for regulating television in the home

the responsibility of the broadcaster

what ACT does to bring about change and how others can join the effort

These topics can be discussed in a variety of ways.

1. Several short 16mm color films that cover the issues surrounding children's television are available for rental. These films can serve as an effective catalyst to an active discussion. (See resource list for suggested films.)

   With or without a film, a certain amount of information should be presented to stimulate discussion. An outline of possible topics follows, with resource suggestions for the discusssion leader.

2. Another method for covering the topics is to divide the large

group into small groups, assigning to each an issue for discussion. A spokesperson from each small group can then report the group's point of view when the total group reconvenes for a general discussion. A debate can also be constructed around any of the issues on children and television.

3. Drawing on local people for a panel discussion is an excellent way to attract an audience. A teacher, librarian, interested parent, physician, dentist, nutritionist, school psychologist, or local broadcaster can create an atmosphere conducive to an exciting follow-up dialogue.

4. A questionnaire about the television viewing habits of children and their families can be used to raise the consciousness of the group. Include questions about the amount of time spent viewing TV, the products advertised on children's TV, the view of the world TV presents to the child, family TV limits, products children ask their parents to buy, and the amount of adult programming a child watches (see questionnaire included in Appendix F).

5. A quiz about television is another way to acquaint people with what they *don't* know about it. The quiz found in this book (see pp. 3–5) can be adapted for use with any group, or a quiz can be made up from the facts found in the program outline. Ask questions about the amount of time a child watches TV, what is advertised on children's TV, how many American homes have a television set, and so on.

Whichever method of discussion is chosen, local television information should be included. For instance: which ACT award winners are shown locally—and when? What do the local stations show children in the late afternoons? What preschool programs are shown locally? Is there a TV column in the local paper, and does it ever include information about children's programs and specials? What local children's events provide alternatives to TV watching? Are there other Saturday morning activities in the community besides TV? Make sure a list of the local stations' addresses is provided, and encourage people to write and express their views and concerns about children's programs.

F. OUTLINE FOR A PROGRAM ON CHILDREN AND TELEVISION

Introduction

1. How much television do children watch? Some facts you may want to point out include:

By the time most children finish high school, they have spent fifteen thousand hours watching television as opposed to eleven thousand hours in school.

Children watch an average of twenty-five to thirty hours of television a week.

The only activity that occupies more of a child's time than TV is sleep.

97 percent of American homes have at least one television set, and many children have a set in their rooms.

2. Dr. Richard Granger, associate professor of clinical pediatrics at Yale University's Child Study Center, has stated: "For a large number of children, television is society at large . . . its messages arrive with the implied sanction both of parents who allow the child to watch and of the larger adult world which obviously prepares and transmits it."[1]

Violence

1. Researchers have considered the following possible effects of television violence. Some points to consider:

Imitation: children may imitate what they see. Children's play is TV-play and children may be learning violent behavior they would not have been exposed to otherwise.

Desensitization: children may become desensitized to real-life violence. The barrage of violent action on television may lessen the impact of real-life conflicts.

Victimization: some children may identify with the victim of television crimes rather than the aggressor. As a result, children may perceive the world as a more violent place than it really is.

2. Dr. Aimée Dorr, educator and child psychologist, points out

that TV often does not reflect reality, but rather presents a fictitious social system in which

criminals are always caught

minorities and the elderly are rarely seen

guilty people always break down under a good lawyer's barrage of questions

problems are solved in an hour

things usually work out for the best

3. Violence=Excitement=Ratings: violence on television has been used to draw large audiences of children. Broadcasters are primarily concerned with the amount of money they can charge advertisers for commercial time, based on the rating for the program.

4. "It is ACT's opinion that the problems with children's television viewing are not merely that the numbers of violent incidents per hour are so many, but that the opportunities to select something different are so few." (*ACT News,* Summer 1976).

Cultural Violence (ageism, sexism, racism)

1. Since children have few real-life experiences to bring to television viewing, they often assume that television depicts society as it is. Consequently, it is important that children's television avoid stereotyping women and cultural and ethnic minorities. Some important points are:

Stereotypes of women and minorities are seen in commercials and programs.

Saturday morning programming still includes many stereotypes of women and minorities.

A large majority of the characters on Saturday morning TV are white. Dr. Chester Pierce of Harvard's Graduate School of Education points out that an animal is more likely to have a speaking role than a black person on Saturday morning shows.

The problem of stereotyping is especially evident in the old reruns recycled for children in the late afternoons on independent stations. (Check local listing for programs of this type.)

Advertising

1. In addition to program messages, children are staying tuned for other messages—the commercials.

   Since children watch over five hours of advertising a week, they see approximately twenty thousand commercials a year.

   Advertisers spend close to $600 million a year selling to children on television.

   The child becomes the advertiser's representative in the home.

2. Are children the proper target for advertising techniques? Research has shown the following:

   Many young children cannot distinguish TV commercials from TV programs.

   Many children believe that all commercials are true.

   Many children do not understand the function of advertising in society.

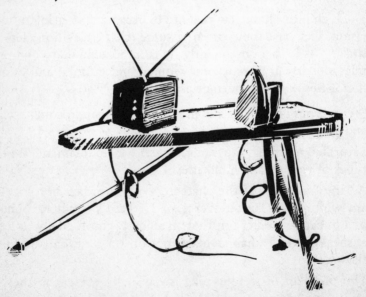

Many children don't understand advertising techniques (premiums, disclaimers, camera techniques).

Many older children develop cynicism about commercial messages.

While we may be training skeptical young consumers, are we also suggesting to our children that deception is an approved strategy in the marketplace, that they are entering a world where manipulation and misrepresentation go hand in hand with making a profit?

3. What are children learning about nutrition from commercials on children's TV?

More than half of the food ads on children's TV are for heavily sugared foods.

Food ads on children's programs are primarily for presweetened cereals and snack foods.

Less than 4 percent of the food ads directed to children are for meat, bread, fruits, vegetables, or dairy products.

4. Why are these ads a problem?

In the United States the average yearly consumption of sugar is over one hundred pounds per person.

98 percent of the population in America suffers from tooth decay.

TV Is a Joint Responsibility of Parents and Broadcasters

1. Broadcasters have a responsibility to provide programs in the public interest, convenience, and necessity, and part of that public interest responsibility is programming for children.

The Supreme Court stated in 1969: "It is the right of the viewers and listeners, not the right of the broadcasters which is paramount."

2. Parents have a responsibility, since many children are watching television during adult viewing hours. The 1977 Nielsen figures indicated:

Less than 20 percent of a child's television viewing time is spent watching Saturday morning programs designed for children.

Almost half of a child's viewing time consists of prime time programs.

Over 10.5 million children are still watching television at 9:00 P.M. on weeknights, and almost a million children are still watching at midnight.

3. Parents can establish television viewing habits in their homes by using guidelines.

ACT has developed a set of guidelines in poster form called *Treat TV with T.L.C.* (see page 65).

Talk about TV with your child.

Look at TV with your child.

Choose TV programs with your child.

ACT Annual Achievement Awards are given to broadcasters who have made significant contributions to children's television (see page 183). Check your local TV guide for times of programs listed.

Changing Children's TV

1. Write letters to the Federal Communications Commission, Federal Trade Commission, networks, advertisers, and local stations. Let them know what you think is good and bad. Send ACT copies of your letters if you can. (See list of addresses, pp. 193–196, and be sure to add local addresses to this list.)

2. Join *Action for Children's Television.*

ACT is a nonprofit national consumer organization based in Newtonville, Mass., working to improve broadcast practices related to children. Through legal action, education, and research, the group is trying to reduce violence and commercialism and encourage quality and diversity on children's television. (See *ACTFACTS* for specific information about ACT's goals, accomplishments, works in progress, and publications.)

ACT has had some major successes:

Advertising time on weekend children's programs has been reduced by 40 percent.

Hosts of children's shows no longer sell products.

Vitamin pills and fireworks can no longer be advertised directly to children on television.

There is more diversity in program content on children's shows.

An ACT membership costs $15 and includes ACT's news magazine *re:act* which keeps members up-to-date on ACT and on the issues surrounding children and television.
Write to ACT for more information:

Action for Children's Television
46 Austin Street
Newtonville, Mass. 01260

(A sign-up sheet with names and addresses may be sent to ACT and information will be sent to those listed.)

NOTE

[1] Richard Granger, *Who Is Talking to Our Children?*, p. 8.

Appendix A: A Short Course in Broadcasting*

A SHORT COURSE IN BROADCASTING   1978

There were 8,408 radio stations operating in the United States at the end of 1977. Of these, 4,508 were commercial AM's, 2,986 were commercial FM's and 914 were noncommercial FM's. There were 996 operating television stations: 516 commercial VHF's, 211 commercial UHF's, 111 noncommercial VHF's and 158 noncommercial UHF's. Most commercial TV's are network-affiliated; approximately 91 operate as independents.

No single entity may own more than seven stations in each service (AM, FM or TV). In TV, no more than five may be VHF. No owner may have two stations of the same service in the same community. No owner of three VHF's in the top fifty markets may purchase other VHF's in the top fifty without a showing of compelling public interest. Newspaper owners may no longer purchase broadcast properties in the same market, nor may radio staion owners acquire TV stations there, nor TV owners radio outlets. TV stations may no longer acquire cable TV franchises in the same city, and networks may not own cable systems at all.

In 1976, the last year for which official FCC figures are available, commercial broadcasting had total revenues of $7.2 billion. Profits were $1.4 billion. Television accounted for $5.2 billion (72.0%) of revenues and $1.25 billion (87.5%) of profits; radio, for $2.0 billion (28.0%) and $178 million (12.5%). Public broadcasting had a 1976 income of $412.1 million—27.6% from the federal government.

There are more than 71.6 million U.S. homes (97% of all homes) with television sets, about 47% of which have more than one set. About 54 million sets are color. It is estimated that about 92% of TV homes can receive UHF signals, and that about 15% are linked with cable systems, according to Arbitron Television. There are an estimated 425 million radio sets in the U.S., 310 million (72.9%) of them in homes and 115 million (27.1%) out of homes.

*Reprinted, with permission, from the *Broadcasting Yearbook 1978.*

The average American home watches TV for six hours and four minutes a day, according to A. C. Nielsen statistics. And the latest study by the Roper Organization (commissioned by the Television Information Office) shows that 64% of the U.S. public turns to TV as the source of most of its news, and that 51% ranks it as the most believable news source.

The average 30-second prime-time network television announcement now costs $50,000 (the highest cost to date, for the first television broadcast of the film "Gone With the Wind," was $130,000; low-rated spots average about $20,000). An estimated 75 million people watched the 1978 Super Bowl telecast. Minute announcements during that event cost $288,000. Thirty-second announcements on individual TV stations range from $15,000 in top-rated specials in major markets to as low as $5 in the second-hundred markets. Radio spots cost from $275 or more in major markets to less than a dollar in small towns.

In 1976, the three television networks had revenues of $2,117,500,000, their fifteen owned and operated TV stations added another $486,900,000, all other stations together contributed $2,594,100,000, for an industry revenue total of $5,198,500,000.

At the same time, the networks had expenses of $1,821,900,000, their fifteen owned stations had expenses of $327,900,000, all other stations together had expenses of $1,798,500,000, for an industry expenses total of $3,948,300,000.

That produced network profits of $295,600,000, up 41.8 percent from 1975, owned-station profits of $159,000,000, up 50.4 percent from 1975, profits for all other stations of $795,600,000, up 70.7 percent from 1975, and all-industry profits of $1,250,200,000, up 60.3 percent over 1975.

The Total Figures for Television in 1976: Revenues, Expenses and Profits*

	1976	1975[†]	% Increase 1975–1976
Broadcast Revenues[1]			
3 networks	2,117,500,000	1,673,800,000	26.5
15 network owned-and-operated stations (all VHF)	486,900,000	395,600,000	23.1

*Reprinted with permission, from *Broadcasting*, August 29, 1977.

[†]Revised from previous report.

All other stations			
477 VHF[2]	2,231,100,000	1,762,200,000	26.6
177 UHF[3]	363,000,000	262,600,000	38.2
Subtotal	2,594,100,000	2,024,700,000	28.1
INDUSTRY TOTAL	5,198,500,000	4,094,100,000	27.0
Broadcast Expenses			
3 networks	1,821,900,000	1,465,300,000	24.3
15 network owned- and-operated stations (all VHF)	327,900,000	290,000,000	13.1
All other stations			
477 VHF[2]	1,500,400,000	1,306,100,000	14.9
188 UHF[3]	298,200,000	252,700,000	18.0
Subtotal	1,798,500,000	1,558,800,000	15.4
INDUSTRY TOTAL	3,948,300,000	3,314,100,000	19.1
Broadcast income (before federal income tax)			
3 networks	295,600,000	208,500,000	41.8
15 network owned- and-operated stations (all VHF)	159,000,000	105,700,000	50.4
All other stations			
477 VHF[2]	730,700,000	456,100,000	60.2
188 UHF[3]	64,800,000	9,900,000	557.1
Subtotal	795,600,000	465,900,000	70.7
INDUSTRY TOTAL	1,250,200,000	780,000,000	60.3

[1] Net, after commissions to agencies, representatives and brokers, and after cash discounts.

[2] The 477 VHF stations represent 496 operations including 19 satellite stations that filed a combined report with their parent stations. The 1975 data reflects 477 VHF stations representing 498 including 21 satellites that filed a combined report with their parent stations.

[3] The 188 UHF stations represent 190 operations including two satellites that filed a combined report with their parent stations. The 1975 data reflect 177 UHF stations representing 180 operations including three satellites that filed a combined report with their parent stations.

Notes: Last digits may not add to total because of rounding. The above station counts do not include four religious stations and three delinquents.

A 10-year TV Track Record*

	Broadcast revenues, expenses and income			Gross advertising revenues		
Year	Total[1] ($ million)	Network[2] ($ million)	National spot[3] ($ million)	Local[4] ($ million)	Revenues[5] ($ million)	Expenses ($ million)	Income[6] ($ million)
1976	$6,029.3	$2,674.9	$1,922.6	$1,431.9	$5,198.5	$3,948.3	$1,250.2
1975 (Rev)	4,722.1	2,156.7	1,449.2	1,116.2	4,094.1	3,313.8	780.3
1974	4,356.6	2,005.6	1,337.3	1,013.7	3,781.5	3,043.2	738.3
1973	4,002.1	1,839.7	1,230.2	932.2	3,464.8	2,811.7	653.1
1972	3,675.0	1,687.5	1,177.4	810.1	3,179.4	2,627.3	552.2
1971	3,178.8	1,490.4	1,022.8	665.6	2,750.3	2,361.2	389.2
1970	3,242.8	1,551.1	1,102.6	589.1	2,808.2	2,354.4	453.8
1969	3,235.5	1,569.6	1,119.1	546.8	2,796.2	2,242.6	553.6
1968	2,916.1	1,424.3	1,009.8	482.0	2,520.9	2,026.1	494.8
1967	2,634.4	1,359.1	882.7	392.6	2,275.4	1,860.8	414.6
1966	2,557.6	1,302.4	882.2	373.0	2,203.0	1,710.1	492.9

[1] Gross advertising revenues are the total amounts paid by advertisers for the use of broadcast facilities. They include commissions paid to advertising agencies and representative agencies, and cover charges for broadcast time and programs, materials, facilities and services supplied by the broadcast industry in connection with the sale of time.

[2] Network advertising revenues for years prior to 1969 were derived as follows: Sales of programs, materials, facilities and service made in connection with sales of time were divided by .85 to yield a figure which included advertising agency commissions. The result of this calculation was added to network time sales (before commissions) to arrive at the total network advertising revenues.

[3] National and regional advertising revenues for years prior to 1969 were estimated with the help of data obtained for the first time in 1969. These provided information on the precise amounts of broadcasting revenues derived from (1) the sale of time to advertisers, including charges for programs, materials and facilities and service supplied in connection with sales of time; and (2) all other broadcast revenues. In prior years, figures reported as "all other broadcast revenues" included some charges for programs, talent, materials and facilities supplied in connection with sales of time. The amounts of the latter to be included in gross advertising revenues were estimated for years prior to 1969 by applying the ratios of advertiser-connected non-time sales to total non-time sales prevailing in 1969. In addition, because stations are not consistent in the way they classify national/regional versus local sales, year to year comparisons in these categories should be made with caution.

[4] Local advertising revenues for years prior to 1969 were derived in the same fashion as described in footnote three.

[5] Gross advertising revenues plus all other broadcast revenues less commissions.

[6] Before federal income tax.

*Reprinted, with permission, from *Broadcasting,* August 29, 1977.

Appendix B: Violence in Children's Television Programs*

EXAMPLES OF VIOLENCE IN THE STORIES

Human Violence With Weapons

Humorous Contexts (Comedy Drama)

"Shish-ka-Bugs" (Bugs Bunny)—Cook threatens Bugs Bunny with a meat cleaver (cook is human).

"Bewitched Bunny" (Bugs Bunny)—Witch chases Bugs Bunny with a cleaver (witch is human).

"Rapid Romance" (Ricochet Rabbit)—Guns are fired; their bullets turn into mallets that hit Rabbit over the head.

"Royal Rhubarb" (Yippee Yappee and Ya Hooey)—Spears hurled at king, swords thrown at knight, bombs thrown, knight and guards shot out of cannon, king shot with slingshot and sent underwater with dynamite.

"Steal Wool" (Looney Tunes)—Cannon, lever, and slingshot used by Ralph, who is injured by slingshot.

"Southern Fried Rabbit" (Bugs Bunny)—Yosemite Sam shoots at Bugs, Sam is blasted with a cannon.

"Gone Batty" (Merry Melodies)—Catcher breaks bat over runner's head. Players are hit with the ball, causing four bumps on the head.

"Zipping Along" (Roadrunner)—Bird and coyote considered animals, since they don't speak or exhibit human characteristics. Hand grenade explodes in coyote's mouth, coyote is caught in mouse trap he set for roadrunner, coyote launches himself with kite and bomb, exploding when he hits ground. TNT explodes, rifles fire at coyote, wrecker ball intended for bird falls on coyote.

"Zero Hero" (Touché Turtle and Dum Dum)—Touché stabs gorilla with sword.

*Reprinted from *Children's Television: An Analysis of Programming and Advertising Practices* by F. Earle Barcus with Rachel Wolkin. Copyright © 1977 by Praeger Publishers, Inc. Reprinted by permission of Holt, Rinehart, and Winston.

"Hook, Line and Stinker" (Roadrunner)—Sledgehammer's loose head hits coyote, dynamite trap intended for bird explodes on coyote, cannonball lands on coyote's head.

"Like Wild Man" (Touché Turtle and Dum Dum)—Saturday is hit over head with club and gun is stolen. Saturday shoots at Crusoe. Wild man threatened with sword, turtle is machine-gunned.

"Porky's Romance" (Porky Pig)—Petunia hits Porky over head with a rolling pin.

"Genie with the Light Pink Fur" (New Pink Panther Show)—PP is hit with hockey stick by kid on skate board.

Addams Family—Addams Family goes to Indianapolis Speedway. In car race between Count Evil and Flash Jorden, the Count uses a high-powered arrow to puncture the gas tank of his competitor. Violence intended to foil Flash's chance of winning the race. No bodily injury was inflicted.

"Ugly Duckling" (Mel-O-Tunes)—Shotguns shoot at ducks (represented as animals).

"Daniel Boone" (Mel-O-Tunes)—Daniel Boone shoots in a hunting scene and throws a knife.

"Laugh-a-Loaf" (Lippy the Lion)—Hardy hits Lippy over the head with a club.

"Heading Nome" (Bailey's Comets)—Clues of bones are shot by opponents of Comets. Ray gun is used to destroy the temple clue—violence is used to destroy clues rather than to harm people.

"Kenya Catch That Clue" (Bailey's Comets)—Giant brick used to crash car, elevator crashes, glue is used to coat team and slow them up. Much of the violence is implied rather than shown, and it is directed at foiling the Comet's chances of winning, not at the members themselves.

Wheelie and the Chopper Bunch—Motorcycle gang erects roadblock to stop Wheelie and prevent him from passing road test; Chopper Bunch is smashed at police roadblock.

Rocky and His Friends—Boris uses a "goof gas" gun on guard.

"5, 4, 3, 2, 1, or the Quick Launch Counter" (Rocky and His Friends)—Boris uses "goof gas" gun, missiles drop on Potsylvania. Rocky loses his fur as a result of "goof gas" and scientists become goofy.

"Dudley Do-Right of the Mounties" (Rocky and His Friends)—Nasty Noogle uses a gun, bomb, and axe. Violence is directed at Inspector Fenwick.

Flintstones—Wilma bangs Fred over head with frying pan and hits Hot Lips on head with her pocketbook.

"Hamlet on Rye" (Mr. Magoo)—Plane crashes, cat is caught in a trap and vase falls on its head. Magoo beats cat on head with broom for causing damage.

"Tycoon Land" (Mr. Magoo)—Magoo hits walrus over the head with wrench.

"Night Fright" (Mr. Magoo)—Cicero is spun through a washing machine, hit over the head with a bat, slips on a banana peel, and is shot by Magoo when he is mistaken for a prowler.

"Hoots and Saddles" (Lippy the Lion)—Lippy tries to capture an escaping horse that is to perform in a contest. He tries to rope him, fails, and crashes; tries a jet-powered pogo stick, drills himself into the ground, and blows himself up with dynamite (horse is animal).

"Raw Raw Rooster" (Merry Melodies)—Foghorn tries to avoid contact with old school chum, Rodh Island. Foghorn squirts him, sets up a punching camera, shooting camera, exploding casava melon, and exploding golf ball—which all backfire and blow up in Foghorn's face.

"The Foxy Wolf" (Nutty Squirrel)—Barnyard animals shoot at foxy wolf.

"Sheepy Wolf" (Nutty Squirrel)—Ricochet and Chavez shoot guns.

"A Horse for Dinner" (Nutty Squirrel)—Horse reroutes banister, which propels blacksmith through roof.

Gilligan's Island—Imposter hits Howell over head with coconut and knocks him out.

Action-Adventure Drama

Lassie's Rescue Rangers—Building is dynamited in bank robbery. Science lab is dynamited and robots killed.

Speed Buggy—Freeze ray and snowball shooter are used to capture car and crew; robots melt.

Violence Without Weapons

Humorous Context (Comedy Drama)

"Who's Kitten Who?" (Bugs Bunny)—Baby Kangaroo is delivered to Sylvester's house in crate—it uses its fists and feet to kick its way out. (Kangaroo depicted as animal.) Sylvester and Kangaroo fight each other. Sylvester is beaten up.

Hong Kong Phooey—"In-nose" man attempts to drown brothers of mystery man.

"Bachelor Buttons" (Wally Gator)—Ella Gator punches Wally, grabs his tail and smashes him, then does the same to a lion.

"Porky's Prize Horse" (Porky Pig)—Clumsy horse crashes through window while jumping.

"Piccadilly Circus" (Pink Panther Show)—Wife slips on items on floor and falls with her bundles.

"Science Friction" (Pink Panther Show)—Anteater is thrown out of laboratory, against tree, and nose is battered. Anteater is kicked (anteater is animal).

Goober—Captain Ahoy captures smugglers.

Sigmund and the Sea Monsters—Sea monsters drag off Sigmund with their tentacles.

"What a Night for a Knight" (Scooby Doo, Where Are You?)—Knight attempts to punch, damages picture.

"Rapid Romance" (Ricochet Rabbit)—Slap Jack Rabbit makes punching bag out of Rabbit; twists his foot and hits him.

"Royal Rhubarb" (Yippee Yappee and Ya Hooey)—Kings hits tower. Knight smashes guard and kings.

"Steal Wool" (Looney Tunes)—Sam punches Ralph every time he tries to steal a sheep.

"Gone Batty" (Merry Melodies)—Goon punches umpire.

"Zero Hero" (Touché Turtle and Dum Dum)—Bong is gorilla who escaped from circus. Touché Turtle in attempt to capture Bong is smashed in his hands.

"Like Wild Man" (Touché Turtle)—Woman jumps from burning building and crashes turtle into ground.

"Genie with the Light Pink Fur" (New Pink Panther Show)—PP is kicked while he is in Aladdin's lamp becoming a genie. PP is burned with hot water and thrown in a city dump.

"Heading Nome" (Bailey's Comets)—Tail of whale hits entire Comets team.

"Kenya Catch That Clue" (Bailey's Comets)—Lion attacks hero (not actually seen). Bees attack bears.

"Foxy Wolf" (Nutty Squirrel)—Clara is carried in jaws of foxy wolf.

"Our Gang in Farm Hands" (Little Rascals)—Froggy thrown off horse, falls on ground.

I Love Lucy—Boy for whom Lucy is baby-sitting kicks her in the shins several times.

Action-Adventure Drama

"Else When" (Land of the Lost)—Monsters try to strangle Dad and Will, then tie them up.

Natural Violence
Humorous Context

Fat Albert and the Cosby Kids—Thurin falls off things by accident and hurts himself.

"Heading Nome" (Bailey's Comets)—A waterfall pours over the team, which is trapped in a snowball.

My Favorite Martian—Brennan gets an electric shock. Glider plane crashes through window, into door and rain barrel.

"Fulton's Folly" (U.S. of Archie)—Two explosions in science lab, several ships sink.

"Hook, Line and Stinker" (Roadrunner)—Coyote is struck by lightning.

"5, 4, 3, 2, 1, or the Quick Launch Counter" (Rocky and His Friends)—Hot air singes Rocky's fur.

"Hook and Ladder" (Little Rascals)—Fire in barn. Dynamite is thrown out window and explodes.

Action-Adventure Drama

"The Magics of Megas-Tu" (Star Trek)—Winds and lightning rock the Enterprise, slightly injuring crew; Kirk falls and hurts his head.

Run Joe Run—Fire results in child being burned.

Emergency Plus Four—Tornado whips through town. Old man's arm injured while he is escaping from the shack that fell because of the storm.

Shazam—Rattlesnake poisons Danny and he is trapped by falling rock slide.

Appendix C:
ACT Achievement
Awards

ACT's Achievement in Children's Television Awards are presented annually to broadcasters who have made "a significant contribution toward improving children's television."

In addition, ACT initiated a Corporate Honor Roll in 1976 to recognize those corporations who have made a "major commitment to underwrite children's television programs without commercial interruptions."

ACT ACHIEVEMENT IN CHILDREN'S TELEVISION AWARDS, 1977

National Achievement Awards were given to:

- ABC-TV, for the "Weekend Specials," for adding quality children's drama to the Saturday morning schedule.
- CBS-TV, for "Fat Albert and the Cosby Kids," for adding a humane sense of humor to Saturday morning television.
- The Corporation for Entertainment and Learning, Inc., for "Marlo and the Magic Movie Machine," for recycling archival newsreels for young viewers who missed them the first time.
- Field Communications, for "Snipets," for using the minutes between programs to soothe the pains of growing up.
- South Carolina ETV, for "Studio See," a series as exciting as all outdoors.
- Walt Disney Productions, for "The New Mickey Mouse Club," for presenting the best of Disney animation in an upbeat, up-to-date format.
- WGBH-TV, Boston, for "Captioned ZOOM!" for making "ZOOM!" more meaningful for hearing-impaired children.

183

Local Achievement Awards winners were:

- WIIC-TV, Pittsburgh, for "Catercousins," a weekly program which encourages children to recognize their own talents as creators.
- WRC-TV, Washington, D.C., for "The Beth and Bower Half Hour," a delightful program of food, fun, and fantasy.
- WSB-TV, Atlanta, for "Super 2," for bringing the community to children and children to the community.
- WTTW-TV, Chicago, for "As*We*See*It," for its honest and forthright examination of problems relating to school integration.

Awards for mini-series were given to:

- CBS News, for "Razzmatazz," a weekly children's magazine produced with a creative flair.
- Daniel Wilson Productions, for "Little Vic," for its sensitive adaptation of a children's literary classic.
- Unicorn Tales, Inc., for "Unicorn Tales," for introducing young viewers to the world of musical theatre.
- WMT-TV, Cedar Rapids, for "Festival Iowa," for enticing young viewers to explore local arts experiences.

ACT Commendations for continuing excellence were given to:

- ABC, for the "ABC Afterschool Specials."
- ABC News, for "Animals Animals Animals."
- The Behrens Company, Miami, for "Kidsworld."
- KOMO-TV, Seattle, for "Boomerang."
- Multimedia, for "Young People's Specials."
- NBC, for "Special Treat."
- WGBH-TV, Boston, for "Rebop."
- WQED-TV, Pittsburgh, for "Once Upon a Classic."

A special award was given to the Westinghouse Broadcasting Company for the "outstanding commitment to local children's programming" which has been made by its owned stations.

Corporate Honor Roll Awards were given to:

- Allied Chemical Corporation, for underwriting "Music."

* Exxon U.S.A. Foundation, for underwriting "Villa Alegre."
* General Foods, for underwriting "ZOOM!"
* McDonald's Local Restaurants Association, for underwriting "Once Upon a Classic."

ACT ACHIEVEMENT IN CHILDREN'S TELEVISION AWARDS, 1976

* ABC-TV, for the "ABC Afterschool Specials," a dramatic series committed to excellence in the afterschool hours.
* ABC-TV News, for "Animals Animals Animals," a weekly program that enhances the world of science with poetry, myth, and music.
* The Behrens Company, Miami, for "Kidsworld," a national news magazine for children with local contributions from participating stations.
* Educational Development Center, Newton, Mass., for "Infinity Factory," a multicultural look at the world of mathematics.
* KETC-TV, St. Louis, for "Common Cents," a series of miniprograms that explain elementary economics to the TV child.
* KOMO-TV, Seattle, for "Boomerang," a preschool program that uses song and story to ease the process of growing up.
* KRON-TV, San Francisco, for "Kidswatch," a news program that turns public affairs into children's affairs.
* NBC-TV, for "Muggsy," a sensitive weekly dramatization of the problems encountered by inner-city children.
* NBC-TV, for "Special Treat," a once-a-month afterschool program in a variety of formats.
* WGBH-TV, Boston, for "Rebop," a series of portraits of young people from diverse cultural and ethnic backgrounds.
* WMAQ-TV, Chicago, for "Bubblegum Digest," a weekly news program written and hosted by children.
* WQED-TV, Pittsburgh, for "Once Upon a Classic," a dramatic presentation of literary favorites designed for children and their families.
* WSB-TV, Atlanta, for "Operation Education," a series of programs and PSAs designed to promote the importance of going to school.

Corporate Honor Roll Awards, for underwriting children's programs without commercials, went to:

General Foods, for "ZOOM!"

General Mills, Inc., for "Rebop."

ITT, for "Big Blue Marble."

Johnson and Johnson Baby Products Company, for "Mister Rogers' Neighborhood."

McDonald's Local Restaurants Association, for "Once Upon a Classic."

Mobil Oil Corporation, for specials for children and their families.

Sears Roebuck Foundation, for "Mister Rogers' Neighborhood."

A special award was presented to the Public Broadcasting Service (PBS) for its continued commitment to providing a diverse selection of creative programs designed to meet the needs of children of different ages at times when they are watching television. On hand to accept the award was Larry Grossman, president of PBS.

ACT ACHIEVEMENT IN CHILDREN'S TELEVISION AWARDS, 1975

- CBS-TV, for "The CBS Children's Film Festival," a weekly program which presents a diverse sampling of outstanding international films for children.

- CBS-TV News, for "Marshall Efron's Illustrated, Simplified and Painless Sunday School," a creative introduction to Biblical stories.

- Children's Television Workshop, for "The Electric Company," a daily program which presents a positive image of women and racial minorities.

- Robert Keeshan Associates, producers of "Captain Kangaroo," for including original, popular, and classical music selected to delight a preschool audience.

- KLRN-TV, Austin, Texas, for "Carrascolendas," a bilingual program designed to encourage bicultural awareness and enhance the sense of self-worth among English- and Spanish-speaking children.

- NBC-TV, for "GO-USA," a series of historical dramas based on the lives of children and adults who made significant but little-known contributions to the growth of this country.

- Post-Newsweek Stations, for "The Reading Show," a program which combines the use of broadcast and printed materials to improve the reading comprehension and vocabulary levels of elementary-school students through cooperation between a local school system and the station group.

- Taft Broadcasting Company, for "Max B. Nimble," a program which demonstrates the commitment of a station group to meeting the needs of its preschool audience.

* Martin Tahse Productions, for bringing back "Kukla, Fran, and Ollie," a family program which continues to entertain an audience of parents and children after nearly three decades.

* Westinghouse Broadcasting Company, for "Call It Macaroni," an informative adventure series designed to be broadcast in the afterschool and early evening hours.

* WGBH-TV, Boston, for "The Spider's Web," a daily radio storybook which represents a new concept in educational broadcasting in its adaptations of children's classics from a cross-cultural literary tradition.

* WXYZ-TV, Detroit, for "Hot Fudge," a program which makes an important contribution to preventive medicine in the area of mental health by encouraging young viewers to feel good about themselves.

* A special award went to the *Agency for Instructional Television* for developing informative and engaging programs such as "Bread and Butterflies," "Ripples," "Inside Out," and "Self-Incorporated," which are creative learning resources designed to stimulate classroom discussion and foster interpersonal understanding and mutual respect.

ACT ACHIEVEMENT IN CHILDREN'S TELEVISION AWARDS, 1974

* ABC-owned and operated stations for "Over 7," a program in magazine format created specifically for family viewing during early prime time hours.

* Alphaventure, for creating the "Big Blue Marble," an ITT-backed venture designed to run with no commercials; and for developing teacher materials to supplement the program.

* CBS-TV News, for "In the News," a series of brief reports positioned between Saturday morning programs and designed to explain current events making headline news.

* The Chinese Committee for Affirmative Action in San Francisco for "Yut, Yee, Sahm" (Here We Come), a program designed to increase multi-cultural awareness among children.

* The Exxon USA Foundation, for its financial support of "Villa Alegre," a program on the public broadcasting system, designed to meet the needs of children of diverse cultural and linguistic backgrounds.

* Prime Time School Television in Chicago for developing and distribut-

ing timely educational materials about televised prime-time specials and documentaries for teachers' classroom use.

- WBZ-TV, Boston, for developing "Something Else," a program designed for eight- to twelve-year-olds, featuring local children in a constructive alternative to Saturday morning viewing.

- WNET-TV, New York, for offering a two-week festival of quality daytime programming for children during mid-year holiday vacations, with the support of the Heckscher Foundation.

ACT ACHIEVEMENT IN CHILDREN'S TELEVISION AWARDS, 1973

- Sears-Roebuck Foundation, for "Mister Rogers' Neighborhood."

- Xerox Corporation, for the Spanish and Portuguese versions of "Sesame Street."

- Mobil Oil Corporation, for "The Electric Company."

- General Foods, for support to twenty local stations airing "Sesame Street" on Saturdays.

- Quaker Oats, for support to three local stations airing "Sesame Street" on Saturdays.

- IBM, for support of the ballet "Sleeping Beauty," aired when many children were watching.

- Miles Laboratories, Sauter Labs/Hoffman-Laroche, and Bristol-Myers, for withdrawing ads for vitamin pills from TV programs with a majority audience of children.

- Avco and Meredith Broadcasting Corporations, for combining their resources and expertise to produce "meaningful children's TV programming in hours of all-family viewing."

- ABC-TV, for "After School Specials," one hour monthly, proving that it is possible for a network to produce and air a special children's program in the afternoon, and for "Multiplication Rock," animated short segments on mathematics aired during Saturday morning programs.

- CBS-TV News, for "What's an Election All About" and "What's a Convention All About"—two news specials designed for children.

- NBC-TV, for "Watch Your Child," an attempt to produce a daily half-hour program for preschoolers, with limited commercialism.

- Westinghouse Broadcasting Company, for continued commitment to science for children, with limited commercialism, on "Earth Lab" (one hour weekly).

- WCVB-TV, Boston, for commitment by a commercial station to the needs of the community's children, including two locally produced programs—"Jabberwocky" (half-hour daily) and "Young Reporters" (half-hour weekly).

- WMAL-TV, Washington, D.C., for a daily children's program aired with clustered commercials—"The Magic Door" (one hour daily).

- WPIX-TV, New York, for two locally produced children's programs aired with clustered commercials—"Magic Garden" (half-hour weekly) and "Joya's Fun School" (half-hour weekly).

- To the 350,000 children who contributed creative material and ideas to "ZOOM!" (PBS/WGBH-TV), for proving that children can do it even if some commercial broadcasters can't.

- To commercial stations (48) airing "Vision On," for providing the first children's program designed for both deaf and hearing children.

- To commercial stations (44) airing "Sesame Street" without commercials, for showing how commercial television can help children in areas where there is no public television (one hour daily).

- Special mention for outstanding regularly scheduled family programs:
  "The Waltons," CBS-TV (one hour weekly)
  National Geographic Society Specials
  Jacques Cousteau Specials

ACT ACHIEVEMENT IN CHILDREN'S TELEVISION AWARDS, 1972

- Post-Newsweek TV Stations, Washington, D.C., and Florida, for seeking out quality programs for children and for clustering commercials on such programs.

- Hallmark Cards, for sponsoring a sixty-minute dramatic presentation, shown in early evening prime time, when older children would be watching, without any commercial interruptions ("The Snow Goose," NBC-TV, November 15, 1971, 8:00–9:00 P.M.)

- Health Tex (Standard Romper) for outstanding institutional advertising within a children's TV program shown in early evening prime time ("Babar Comes to America," NBC-TV, September 7, 1971, 7:30–8:00 P.M.)

- Children's Television Workshop, for the concept of a creative unit devoted to producing children's television programs and for experimentation in television education for young children.

- Mr. Fred Rogers, for pioneering efforts in meeting the emotional needs of young children through television.
- Mr. Robert Keeshan, for sixteen years of devotion to creative television for preschool children on "Captain Kangaroo," and for ending his personal involvement in selling commercial products on his program in 1972.
- "The Kids' Thing," WHDH-TV, Boston, for providing five special half-hour programs for children during a school vacation week, without commercials (December 27–31, 1971, 9:30–10:00 A.M.).

- Public Broadcasting stations across the country, for presenting a variety and diversity of programs for children, aired at times when many children are watching.

"Mister Rogers' Neighborhood"	(daily)	(network)
"Sesame Street"	(daily)	(network)
"Electric Company"	(daily)	(network)
"Masquerade"	(weekly)	(network)
"ZOOM!"	(weekly)	(network)
"Hodge Podge Lodge"	(daily)	(local)
"What's New"	(daily)	(local)

Commended

Commercial networks and local stations did provide some diversity in the children's programming schedule for the 1971–1972 season. However, many of the new programs were still interrupted by commercials.

Since ACT believes that children's programs should be free of commercialism, the following programs do not meet ACT's criteria for an award, but are commended:

Earth Lab	Group W/ Westinghouse	Saturday, 9:00–10:00 A.M.
Children's Film Festival	CBS-TV	Saturday, 1:00–2:00 P.M.
In the News		Saturday, eight 2-minute items on hour and half hour.
You Are There		Saturday, 12:30–1:00 P.M.
Jackson Five	ABC-TV	Saturday, 9:30–10:00 A.M.
Curiosity Shop		Saturday, 11:00–12 noon
Make a Wish		Sunday, 11:30–12 noon
Take a Giant Step	NBC-TV	Saturday, 11:00–12 noon
Mr. Wizard		Saturday, 12:00–12:30 P.M.

Appendix D:
Resource Directory

Prepared by Jean Johnson

USEFUL ADDRESSES
Government Agencies

Chairman, Consumer Product Safety Commission, 1111 Eighteenth Street NW, Washington, D.C. 20207

Chairman, Federal Communications Commission, 1919 M Street NW, Washington, D.C. 20554

Chairman, Federal Trade Commission, Bureau of Consumer Protection, Pennsylvania Avenue at Sixth Street NW, Washington, D.C. 20580

Director, Food and Drug Administration, Department of Health, Education, and Welfare, 5600 Fishers Lane, Rockville, MD 20857

Both the Senate and the House of Representatives have subcommittees responsible for television and communications. For your information, a complete list of members of those committees follows. Write to them c/o Subcommittee on Communications at either the Senate Office Building or the House Office Building, Washington, D.C.

Senate Committee on Commerce, Science and Transportation
Subcommittee on Communications

Ernest F. Hollings (D., SC), Chairman
Howard W. Cannon (D., NV)
John C. Danforth (R., MO)
John A. Durkin (D., NH)
Wendell H. Ford (D., KY)
Robert P. Griffin (R., MI)
Daniel K. Inouye (D., HI)
Warren G. Magnuson (D., WA)
Bob Packwood (R., OR)

Donald W. Riegle (D., MI)
Harrison H. Schmitt (R., NM)
Ted Stevens (R., AK)
Edward Zorinsky (D., NE)

House Committee on Interstate and Foreign Commerce Subcommittee on Communications

Lionel Van Deerlin (D., CA), Chairman
Charles J. Carney (D., OH)
Louis Frey, Jr. (R., FL)
Albert Gore, Jr. (D., TN)
Thomas A. Luken (D., OH)
Edward J. Markey (D., MA)
Marc L. Marks (R., PA)
Barbara A. Mikulski (D., MD)
W. Henson Moore (R., LA)
Carlos J. Moorhead (R., CA)
John M. Murphy (D., NY)
Martin A. Russo (D., IL)
Henry A. Waxman (D., CA)
Timothy E. Wirth (D., CO)

Networks

Address your letters to the presidents of these companies.
ABC, 1330 Avenue of the Americas, New York, NY 10019,
   (212-581-7777).
CBS, 51 West 52 Street, New York, NY 10019 (212-975-4321).
NBC, 50 Rockefeller Plaza, New York, NY 10020 (212-664-4444).
PBS, 485 L'Enfant Plaza West, Washington, D.C. 20024 (202-488-5000).

Station Groups

Some major groups owning television stations are listed below. Address
your letters to the president.
Avco Broadcasting Corporation, 1600 Provident Tower, Cincinnati, OH
   45202.
Capital Cities Communications, Inc., 24 East 51 Street, New York, NY
   10022.
Cox Broadcasting Corporation, 1601 West Peachtree Street NE, Atlanta,
   GA 30309.
John E. Fetzer Stations, 590 West Maple Street, Kalamazoo, MI 49001.

Forward Communications Corporation, Box 1088, 1114 Grand Avenue, Wausau, WI 54401.

Hearst Stations, 959 Eighth Avenue, New York, NY 10019.

Kaiser Broadcasting Stations, One Hallidie Plaza, 7th floor, San Francisco, CA 94102.

Metromedia Inc., 277 Park Avenue, New York, NY 10017.

Post-Newsweek Stations, Inc., 40th and Brandywine Streets NW, Washington, D.C. 20016.

RKO General Inc., 1440 Broadway, New York, NY 10018.

Scripps-Howard Broadcasting Company, 1100 Central Trust Tower, Cincinnati, OH 45202.

Storer Broadcasting Company, 1177 Kane Concourse, Miami Beach, FL 33154.

Taft Broadcasting Company, 1906 Highland Avenue, Cincinnati, OH 45219.

Tribune Company (*Chicago Tribune*) Stations, 2501 Bradley Place, Chicago, IL 60618.

Westinghouse Broadcasting Company, 90 Park Avenue, New York, NY 10016.

(Complete information available from *Broadcasting Yearbook*, 1735 DeSales Street NW, Washington, D.C. 20036.)

Local Stations

Every local television station has a call sign beginning with "W" east of the Mississippi and with "K" west of the Mississippi. To find the addresses and phone numbers of your local stations, look up the call signs in the phone book under "W" or "K" (WNEW, KRON, etc.). Address your letters to the president of the station.

In addition, station addresses and personnel are listed in *Broadcasting Yearbook.*

Organizations and Groups

Action for Children's Television, 46 Austin Street, Newtonville, MA 02160 (617-527-7870). National nonprofit consumer organization working to encourage diversity and eliminate commercial abuses from children's television. Membership, newsletter, campaigns, research information, film, and library facilities.

Citizens' Communications Center, 1914 Sunderland Place NW, Washington, D.C. 20036 (202-296-4238). Provides legal assistance and advice to citizens interested in taking action in broadcasting area. Publishes annual report.

Council on Children, Media, and Merchandising, 1346 Connecticut Avenue NW, Washington, D.C. 20036 (202-466-2584). The Council, created by Robert Choate, is most active in areas relating to nutrition and food advertising to children.

Media Access Project (MAP), 1910 N Street NW, Washington, D.C. 20036 (202-785-2613). A public-interest law firm practicing regularly before the FCC, federal district courts, and appellate courts.

National Association for Better Broadcasting, P.O. Box 43640, Los Angeles, CA 90043 (213-474-3283). Oldest broadcasting organization. Has membership, publishes newsletter and annual critique of programs on the air.

National Citizens' Committee for Broadcasting, 1028 Connecticut Avenue NW, Suite 402, Washington, D.C. 20036 (202-466-8407). A national organization coordinating citizen efforts in broadcasting. Monitors TV violence and reports on advertisers who sponsor violent programs.

National Congress of Parents and Teachers, 700 Rush Street, Chicago, IL 60611 (312-787-0977). Held regional public hearings on TV violence and publishes lists of the "best" and the "worst" of network programming.

Office of Communication, United Church of Christ, 289 Park Avenue South, New York, NY 10010 (212-475-2121). The Office of Communication spearheads legal efforts to improve minority representation in broadcasting. Publishes materials, gives advice.

Urban Communications Group, 1730 M Street NW, Washington, D.C. 20036. A group involved in minority ownership in broadcasting, especially cable TV.

ACT Contacts

ACT has contacts in the following places. For more information, contact the main ACT office in Newtonville, MA.

Alabama: Auburn
Arkansas: Benton
California: Chico, Los Angeles, Redlands, San Diego, San Francisco
Colorado: Denver
Connecticut: Greenwich, Hartford, New Haven, Weston
District of Columbia
Florida: Coral Gables
Georgia: Atlanta
Hawaii: Makawao
Illinois: Aurora, Chicago, Deerfield, Dekalb
Indiana: Evansville, Indianapolis

Iowa: Cedar Rapids, Des Moines

Maryland: Baltimore, College Park, Silver Spring

Massachusetts: Braintree, Holliston, Marblehead, Sudbury, Wellesley, Worcester

Michigan: Ann Arbor, Birmingham, Detroit, Grand Rapids, Kalamazoo, Lansing, Portage

Minnesota: St. Paul

Mississippi: University

Missouri: Columbia, Des Peres, St. Louis, Union

New Jersey: Cliffside Park, New Brunswick, Pennsauken, Princeton

New York: Albany, Auburn, Binghamton, Brooklyn, Buffalo, Garden City, Larchmont, New York City, Rochester, Syracuse

North Carolina: Raleigh

North Dakota: Fargo

Ohio: Berea, Cincinnati, Cleveland, Cuyahoga Falls, Dayton, Duncan Falls, Lyndhurst

Oklahoma: Tulsa

Oregon: Eugene, Prineville

Pennsylvania: Lancaster, Philadelphia, Pittsburgh, Wilkes-Barre

Rhode Island: Middletown, Newport

Texas: Austin, Big Sandy, San Antonio, Uvalde

Utah: Ogden, Salt Lake City

Virginia: Reston

Washington: Mercer Island, Seattle

West Virginia: Morgantown

Australia

Canada

Japan

Mexico

Virgin Islands

There are also local committees on children's television in the following areas:

Atlanta, Dayton, Denver, Des Moines, Detroit, District of Columbia, Lancaster (PA), Lansing (MI), New York City, Pittsburgh, Rochester (NY), San Francisco, Seattle.

MATERIALS AVAILABLE FROM ACT

ACT Studies

Barcus, F. Earle, *Romper Room: An Analysis.* Prepared for Action for Children's Television, September 1971. 35 pp. $5.00.

——, *Saturday Children's Television: A Report of Television Programming and Advertising on Boston Commercial Television*. Prepared for Action for Children's Television, July 1971. 111 pp. $10.00.

——, *Network Programming and Advertising in the Saturday Children's Hours: A June and November Comparison*. An update of the above study, January 1972. 32 pp. $5.00.

——, *Concerned Parents Speak Out on Children's Television*. A report on the ACT/Parade Magazine quiz. Prepared for Action for Children's Television, March 1973. 95 pp. $10.00.

——, *Television in the Afterschool Hours*. Prepared for Action for Children's Television, November 1975. 78 pp. $10.00.

——, *Weekend Commercial Children's Television*. Prepared for Action for Children's Television, November 1975. 95 pp. $10.00.

——, *Pre-Christmas Advertising to Children*. Prepared for Action for Children's Television, September 1976. 34 pp. $10.00.

——, *Commercial Children's Television on Weekends and Weekday Afternoons*. Prepared for Action for Children's Television, June 1978. 61 pp.; appendices. $25.00.

Jennings, Ralph and Carol, *Programming and Advertising Practices in Television Directed to Children—Another Look*. Prepared for Action for Children's Television, July 1971. 43 pp. $5.00.

Mendelson, Gilbert, and Young, Morissa, *Network Children's Programming: A Content Analysis of Black and Minority Treatment on Children's Television*. Prepared by Black Efforts for Soul in Television for Action for Children's Television, August 1972. 21 pp. $3.50.

Yankelovitch, Daniel, *Mothers' Attitudes Toward Children's Television Programs and Commercials*. Prepared for Action for Children's Television, March 1970. 49 pp. $5.00.

FTC

Testimony of Action for Children's Television Before the Federal Trade

Commission: General Comments on Television Advertising to Children, November 10, 1971. 18 pp. $2.50.

Petition to Prohibit Advertisements for Children's Vitamins on Children's and Family Television Programs, November 10, 1971. 35 pp. $3.50.

Petition to Prohibit Advertisements for Toys on Children's Television Programs, December 15, 1971. 37 pp. $5.00.

Petition to Prohibit Advertisements for Edibles on Children's Television Programs, March 22, 1972; *Supplementary Filing Relating to ACT Petition to Prohibit Advertising of Edibles on Children's Television,* January 1973; and *Complaints on Specific Food Products,* March 1973. 98 pp. $10.00.

Comments on Proposed Guides Concerning Use of Endorsements and Testimonials in Advertisements, March 1973. 14 pp. $2.50.

Comments on Proposed Guides Concerning Use of Premiums on Television Advertisements Directed to Children, September 1974. 22 pp. $3.50.

Reply Comments on Proposed Guides Concerning Use of Premiums on Television Advertising Directed to Children, August 1975 8 pp. $1.00.

Petition to Promulgate a Rule Prohibiting the Advertising of Vitamins on Children's and Family Television Programs and Request for Temporary Injunction by the Federal Trade Commission against Hudson Pharmaceutical Corporation, October 1975. 190 pp. $10.00.

Complaint against Mars, Inc., for Directing Unfair and Misleading Advertising to Children, April 1976. 12 pp. $2.00.

Formal Complaint against Hasbro Industries, Inc., for Failure to Meet Basic Public Interest Obligations with Respect to Advertising Directed to Children, December 1976. 11 pp. $1.50.

Petition to Promulgate a Rule Prohibiting the Advertising of Candy to Children on Television and Formal Complaints Against Mars, Inc., The Nestle Company, Inc., Fox-Cross Candy Company and the Squibb Corporation for Failure to Meet Basic Public Interest Obligations with Respect to Confectionery Advertising Directed to Children, April 1977. 234 pp. $25.00.

Formal Complaint against General Foods Corporation for Directing Unfair and Deceptive Advertising to Children, May 1977. 14 pp. $1.50.

Formal Complaint against the Ralston Purina Company for Utilizing Unfair and Deceptive Advertising Practices in the Television Commercial, Cited Herein, for "Cookie Crisp Cereal," August 1977, 4 pp. $1.00.

FCC

RM 1569, Docket No. 19142
Brief I, Guidelines for Children's Television, April 29, 1970. 29 pp. $3.50.

Brief II, Toys Advertised Deceptively, December 11, 1970. 26 pp. $3.50.

Brief III, Comments, July 2, 1971. 42 pp. $5.00.

Brief IV, Reply Comments, October 1, 1971. 70 pp. $7.50.

Oral Argument on Children's Television, January 8, 1973. 26 pp. $3.50.

Docket No. 19622
Comments of ACT on Proposed Revisions on Prime Time Access Rule, September 1974. 6 pp. $1.00.

Docket No. 19142
Petition of Action for Children's Television for Rulemaking Looking Toward the Elimination of Sponsorship and Commercial Content in Children's Programs, February 1978. 68 pp. $7.50.

ACT Testimony

Testimony Before the U.S. Senate Commerce Committee on Television Violence, March 24, 1972. 11 pp. $1.50.

Testimony Before the U.S. Senate Select Committee on Nutrition and Human Needs, March 6, 1973. 26 pp. $3.50.

Testimony Before the U.S. Senate Commerce Committee Oversight Hearings. March 7, 1974. 16 pp. $2.50.

Testimony Before the U.S. House of Representatives Subcommittee on Communications, July 14, 1975. 18 pp.; appendices. $2.50.

Testimony Before the U.S. House of Representatives Subcommittee on Commerce, Consumer, and Monetary Affairs, February 25, 1976. 14 pp. $2.00.

Testimony Before the U.S. House of Representatives, Subcommittee on Communications, March 2, 1977. 6 pp. $1.00.

ACT Briefs

ACT v. FCC. Petition for Review of a Report and Policy Statement of the Federal Communications Commission, Brief for Petitioner, November 15, 1975. 55 pp. $5.00.

ACT v. FCC. Petition for Review of a Report and Policy Statement of the Federal Communications Commission, Reply Brief for Petitioner, April 30, 1976. 24 pp. $3.00.

ACT Books

Harmonay, Maureen, ed., *Promise and Performance: ACT's Guide to TV Programming for Children; Volume I: Children with Special Needs.* Cambridge, MA: Ballinger Publishing Company, 1977. 255 pp. $6.95 paper; $12.50 hardcover.

Melody, William, *Children's TV: The Economics of Exploitation.* New Haven: Yale University Press, 1973. 164 pp. $3.95 paper.

Other ACT Materials

ACT FACTS. History of the organization and description of current activities. 10 pp. $1.50.

re:act: Action for Children's Television News Magazine (Quarterly). Yearly subscription $15.00; free with membership in ACT.

ACT Information Packet. An introductory packet of ACT materials, $2.00.

ACT Materials: A Resource List. First copy free; additional copies $ .25. *Children and Television: An ACT Bibliography.* $ .50.

ACT Resource Library Reference Sheets. Current bibliographies on specific subjects, $1.00 each.

"Sex Roles Portrayed on TV"
"Social and Cultural Roles Portrayed on Television"
"Children and Television Advertising"
"Children and Television Violence"
(Other subjects in preparation)

Kids for Sale. Prepared for ACT by CinemaGraphics, Inc. A twenty-minute 16mm color film with sound. Film clips from children's programs and commercials. Interviews with children and parents. 1978. To rent: $30.00; to purchase: $285.00

NUTRITION GAMES/JUEGOS DE NUTRICION. A bilingual nutrition poster with games and suggestions for alternative snack foods. November 1976. $2.00.

Treat TV with T.L.C. ACT's guidelines for parents in the form of an 8½″ × 11″ poster. First copy free; additional copies $ .25 each.

It's as Easy as Selling Candy to a Baby. Produced for ACT by What's Up for Kids, Inc., and Jayan Film Productions. An eleven-minute 16mm color film with sound. Film clips of TV food ads directed to children. Discussion of the impact of television advertising on American eating habits. 1977. To rent: $25.00; to purchase: $185.00.

TV Reminder Tag. A colorful tag designed to hang directly from family television sets. Offers practical advice to parents about TV viewing. Available in English or Spanish, $ .25 each.

Appendix E:
Bibliography

TELEVISION: GENERAL

Bandura, Albert. *Aggression: A Social Learning Analysis.* Englewood Cliffs, NJ: Prentice-Hall, Inc., 1973. 390 pp. $15.21 cloth.

Barnouw, Erik. *Tube of Plenty: The Evolution of American Television.* New York: Oxford University Press, 1975. 518 pp. $14.95 cloth.

Brown, Les. *Encyclopedia of Television.* New York: Quadrangle/The New York Times Book Company, Inc., 1977. 492 pp. $20.00 cloth.

———. *Television: The Business Behind the Box.* New York: Harcourt Brace Jovanovich, Inc., 1971. 374 pp. $8.95 cloth; $2.85 paper.

Cline, Victor B., ed. *Where Do You Draw the Line? An Exploration into Media Violence, Pornography, and Censorship.* Provo, UT: Brigham Young University Press, 1974. 365 pp. $9.95 cloth; $6.95 paper.

Cole, Barry, and Oettinger, Mal. *Reluctant Regulators.* Reading, MA: Addison-Wesley Publishing Company, 1978. 288 pp. $10.95 cloth.

Comstock, George et al. *Television and Human Behavior.* Santa Monica, CA: Rand Corporation (R-1746-CF, R-1747-CF, R-1748-CF), 1975. 3 vols. $27.00/set paper.

Diamond, Edwin. *The Tin Kazoo: Television, Politics, and the News.* Cambridge, MA: MIT Press, 1975. 269 pp. $9.95 cloth.

Feshbach, Seymour, and Singer, Robert D. *Television and Aggression.* San Francisco: Jossey-Bass, Inc., 1971. 186 pp. $7.69 cloth.

Friendly, Fred W. *Due to Circumstances Beyond Our Control.* New York: Vintage Books, 1968. 339 pp. $1.95 paper.

The Future of Public Broadcasting. Published with the Aspen Institute Program on Communications and Society. New York: Praeger Publishers, 1976. 372 pp. $17.50 cloth; paper edition available from Aspen Institute, Palo Alto, CA, $6.95.

Gattegno, Caleb. *Towards a Visual Culture: Educating through Television.* New York: Outerbridge & Dienstfrey, 1969. 117 pp. $7.95 cloth. Distributed through E. P. Dutton & Company, New York.

Gerbner, George et al. *Violence Profile No. 8.* Philadelphia: Annenberg School of Communications, University of Pennsylvania, 1977. 109 pp. $12.50 paper.

Goldsen, Rose K. *The Show and Tell Machine.* New York: The Dial Press, 1977. 427 pp. $10.00 cloth.

Greenfield, Jeff. *Television: The First Fifty Years.* New York: Harry Abrams, 1977. 280 pp. $35.00 cloth.

Guimary, Donald L. *Citizens Groups and Broadcasting.* New York: Praeger Publishers, 1975. 170 pp. $14.00 cloth.

Hilliard, Robert L. *Writing for Television and Radio.* 3rd ed. New York: Hastings House, 1976. 461 pp. $16.50 cloth.

Howitt, Dennis, and Cumberbatch, Guy. *Mass Media Violence and Society.* New York: John Wiley & Sons, 1975. 167 pp. $12.50 cloth.

Jennings, Ralph M., and Richard, Pamela. *How to Protect Your Rights in Television and Radio.* New York: Office of Communication, United Church of Christ, 1974. 167 pp. $5.50 paper.

Johnson, Nicholas. *How to Talk Back to Your Television Set.* Boston: Little, Brown and Company, 1970. 228 pp. $5.75 cloth; $.95 paper.

Larsen, Otto N., ed. *Violence and the Mass Media.* New York: Harper & Row, 1968. 310 pp. $4.50 paper.

McLuhan, Marshall. *Understanding Media: The Extensions of Man.* New York: McGraw-Hill, 1964. 364 pp. $1.95 paper.

Macy, John W., Jr. *To Irrigate a Wasteland.* Berkeley: University of California Press, 1974. 186 pp. $6.95 cloth.

Mayer, Martin. *About Television.* New York: Harper & Row, 1972. 433 pp. $10.00 cloth.

Milgram, Stanley, and Shotland, R. Lance. *Television and Anti-Social Behavior.* New York: Academic Press, 1973. 183 pp. $10.00 cloth.

Owen, Bruce M.; Beebe, Jack H.; and Manning, Willard G., Jr. *Television Economics.* Lexington, MA: D. C. Heath and Company, 1974. 218 pp. $15.00 cloth.

Quinlan, Sterling. *The Hundred Million Dollar Lunch.* Chicago: J. Phillip O'Hara, Inc., 1974. 241 pp. $6.95 cloth.

Report of the Committee on the Future of Broadcasting. London: Her Majesty's Stationery Office, 1977. 522 pp. $13.00 paper.

Rivers, William L., and Nyhan, Michael J., eds. *Aspen Notebook on Gov-Handbook on the Media: 1977-79 Edition.* New York: Praeger Publishers, 1977. 438 pp. $22.00 cloth.

Rivers, William L. and Nyhan, Michael J., eds. *Aspen Notebook on Government and the Media.* New York: Praeger, 1973. 192 pp. $15.00 cloth; paper edition available from Aspen Institute, Palo Alto, CA, $3.95.

Shapiro, Andrew O. *Media Access: Your Rights to Express Your Views on Radio and Television.* Boston: Little, Brown and Company, 1976. 297 pp. $8.95 cloth.

Shayon, Robert Lewis. *Parties in Interest: A Citizens' Guide to Improving Television and Radio.* New York: Office of Communications, United Church of Christ, 1974. 28 pp. One booklet free; in quantity, $ .60 each.

Shayon, Robert Lewis. *The Crowd-Catchers: Introducing Television.* New York: Saturday Review Press, 1973. 175 pp. $6.95 cloth.

Smith, Anthony. *The Shadow in the Cave: The Broadcaster, His Audience, and the State.* Urbana: University of Illinois Press, 1973. 351 pp. $8.95 cloth.

Stanley, Robert H., ed. *The Broadcast Industry: An Examination of Major Issues.* New York: Hastings House, 1975. 256 pp. $13.50 cloth; $7.95 paper.

Television as a Cultural Force. New York: Praeger Publishers, 1976. 189 pp. $15.00 cloth; paper edition available from Aspen Institute, Palo Alto, CA, $4.95.

Television as a Social Force: New Approaches to TV Criticism. New York: Praeger Publishers, 1975. 171 pp. $15.00 cloth; paper edition available from Aspen Institute, Palo Alto, CA, $4.95.

Window Dressing on the Set: Women and Minorities in Television. A Report of the United States Commission on Civil Rights. Washington, D.C.: U.S. Government Printing Office, 1977. 181 pp. $3.25 paper.

TELEVISION AND CHILDREN

Barcus, F. Earle. *Children's Television: An Analysis of Programming and Advertising.* New York: Praeger Publishers, 1977, 218 pp. $18.50.

Bever, T. G. et al. "Young Viewers' Troubling Response to TV Ads." *Harvard Business Review* 53:6 (November–December 1975), pp. 109–119.

Bogart, Leo. "Warning: The Surgeon General Has Determined that TV Violence Is Moderately Dangerous to Your Child's Mental Health." *The Public Opinion Quarterly* 36 (Winter 1972–1973), pp. 491–521.

Cater, Douglass, and Strickland, Stephen. *TV Violence and the Child: The Evolution and Fate of the Surgeon General's Report.* New York: Russell Sage Foundation, 1975. 167 pp. Distributed by Basic Books, $6.95 cloth.

"Children's Television Programming and Research." *Phaedrus: An International Journal of Children's Literature Research* 5:1 (Spring 1978). Available from Phaedrus, Inc., Box 1166, Marblehead, MA 01945. $7.50.

Chu, Godwin C., and Schramm, Wilbur. *Learning from Television: What the Research Says.* Rev. ed. Washington, D.C.: National Association of Educational Broadcasters, 1968. 116 pp. $6.00 paper.

Cohen, Dorothy H. "Is TV a Pied Piper?" *Young Children* (November 1974), pp. 4–14.

Cook, Thomas D. et al. *Sesame Street Revisited.* New York: Russell Sage Foundation, 1975. 410 pp. $15.00 cloth.

Drabman, Ronald S. and Thomas, Margaret Hanratty. "Does Watching Violence on Television Cause Apathy?" *Pediatrics* 57:3 (March 1976), pp. 329–331.

"The Ecology of Education: Television." *Principal* 56:3 (January/February 1977), 112 pp. Available from The National Association of Elementary School Principals, 1801 North Moore Street, Arlington, VA 22209. $4.00.

"The Effects of Television on Children and Adolescents: A Symposium." *Journal of Communication* 25:4 (Autumn 1975), pp. 13–101.

Federal Communications Commission. "Children's Television Programs: Report and Policy Statement." *Federal Register* 39:215 (Wednesday, November 6, 1974), Part II, pp. 39396–39409.

The Federal Role in Funding Children's Television Programming. Bloomington, IN: Institute for Communication Research, Indiana University, 1975. 2 vols.

Friedrich, Lynette Kohn, and Stein Aletha Huston. "Aggressive and Prosocial Television Programs and the Natural Behavior of Preschool Children." *Monographs of the Society for Research in Child Development* 38:4 (August 1973). Chicago: University of Chicago Press, 1973. 64 pp. $3.00.

Gussow, Joan. "Counternutritional Messages of TV Ads Aimed at Children." *Journal of Nutrition Education* 4:2 (1972), pp. 48-52.

Harmonay, Maureen, ed. *Promise and Performance: ACT's Guide to TV Programming for Children, Volume I: Children with Special Needs.* Cambridge, MA: Ballinger Publishing Company, 1977. 255 pp. $12.50 cloth; $6.95 paper.

Himmelweit, Hilde; Oppenheim, A. N.; and Vince, Pamela. *Television and the Child.* Reprint of Chapters 1-4. London: Oxford University Press, 1958. 52 pp. Available from Television Information Office, 745 5th Avenue, New York, NY 10022.

Kids, Food and Television: The Compelling Case for State Action. New York State Assembly, 1977. 87 pp.

Lange, David L.; Baker, Robert K.; and Ball, Sandra J. *Mass Media and Violence: A Report to the National Commission on the Causes and Prevention of Violence.* Vol. XI. Washington, D.C.: U.S. Government Printing Office, 1969. 614 pp. $2.50 paper.

Leifer, Aimée Dorr; Gordon, Neal J.; and Graves, Sherryl Browne. "Children's Television: More Than Mere Entertainment." *Harvard Educational Review* 44:2 (1974), pp. 213-245.

Lesser, Gerald S. *Children and Television: Lessons from Sesame Street.* New York: Random House, 1974. 290 pp. $10.00 cloth.

Liebert, Robert M.; Neale, John M.; and Davidson, Emily S. *The Early Window: Effects of TV on Children and Youth.* New York: Pergamon Press, 1973. 133 pp. $9.50 cloth; $6.50 paper.

Melody, William H. *Children's Television: The Economics of Exploitation.* New Haven: Yale University Press, 1973. 164 pp. $7.95 cloth; $1.95 paper.

Noble, Grant. *Children in Front of the Small Screen.* Beverly Hills, CA: Sage Publications, 1975. 256 pp. $15.00 cloth.

Polsky, Richard M. *Getting to Sesame Street.* New York: Praeger Publishers, 1974. 139 pp. $12.50 cloth; paperback edition available from Aspen Institute, Palo Alto, CA, $3.95.

Public Broadcasting and Education. A Report to the Corporation for Public Broadcasting from the Advisory Council of National Organizations. Washington, D.C.: Corporation for Public Broadcasting, 1975. 114 pp.

Research on the Effects of Television Advertising on Children. Report prepared for the National Science Foundation. Washington, D.C.: U.S. Government Printing Office, 1977. 229 pp. $3.75 paper.

Rutstein, Nat. *"Go Watch TV!" What and How Much Should Children Really Watch?* New York: Sheed and Ward, 1974. 213 pp. $6.95 cloth.

Schramm, Wilbur; Lyle, Jack; and Parker, Edwin B. *Television in the Lives of Our Children*. Stanford: Stanford University Press, 1961. 324 pp. $8.50 cloth, $2.95 paper.

Stein, Aletha Huston, and Friedrich, Lynette Kohn. *Impact of Television on Children and Youth*. Chicago: University of Chicago Press, 1975. 72 pp. $2.50 paper.

Television and Growing Up: The Impact of Televised Violence. Report to the Surgeon General, United States Public Health Service from the Surgeon General's Scientific Advisory Committee on Television and Social Behavior. Washington, D.C.: U.S. Government Printing Office, 1972. 279 pp. ERIC Document ED 057 595.

Television and Social Behavior. A Technical Report of the Surgeon General's Advisory Committee on Television and Social Behavior. 5 vols. Washington, D.C.: U.S. Government Printing Office, 1972. ERIC Documents ED 059 623–627.

Ward, Scott; Wackman, Daniel B.; and Wartella, Ellen. *How Children Learn to Buy*. Beverly Hills, CA: Sage Publications, 1977. 268 pp. $6.95 paper.

Williams, Frederick, and Van Wart, Geraldine. *Carrascolendas: Bilingual Education through Television*. New York: Praeger Publishers, 1974. 229 pp. $16.50 cloth.

Winn, Marie. *The Plug-In Drug*. New York: Viking Press, 1977. 231 pp. $8.95 cloth.

PERIODICALS: GENERAL

Advertising Age. Advertising Publications, Inc., 740 Rush Street, Chicago, IL 60611. Weekly, $12.00/year.

Broadcasting. Broadcasting Publications, 1735 DeSales Street N.W., Washington, D.C. 20036. Weekly, $25.00/year.

Cablelines. Cablecommunications Resource Center, 1900 L Street N.W., Washington, D.C. 20036. Bimonthly, $5.00/year.

Journal of Advertising Research. Advertising Research Foundation, 3 East 54 Street, New York, NY 10022. Bimonthly, $30.00/year.

Journal of Broadcasting. Broadcast Education Association, 1771 N Street N.W., Washington, D.C. 20036. Quarterly, $17.50/year.

Journal of Communication. Annenberg School of Communications, PO Box 13358, Philadelphia, PA 19101. Quarterly, $15.00/year.

Journal of Consumer Research. American Marketing Association, 222 South Riverside Plaza, Chicago, IL 60606. Quarterly, $12.50/year.

Mass Media Newsletter. Mass Media Ministries, Inc., 2116 North Charles Street, Baltimore, MD 21218. Biweekly, $10.00/year.

Media Report to Women. Media Report to Women, 3306 Ross Place N.W., Washington, D.C. 20008. Monthly, $15.00/year.

Notes from the Center. Cable Television Information Center, 2100 M Street N.W., Washington, D.C. Quarterly, free.

Public Telecommunications Review. National Association of Educational Broadcasters, 1346 Connecticut Avenue N.W., Washington, D.C. 20036. Bimonthly, $18.00/year.

TV Guide. Triangle Publications, Inc., Box 400, Radnor, PA 19088. Weekly, $12.00/year.

Television Quarterly. National Academy of Television Arts and Sciences, 291 South LaCienega Boulevard, Beverly Hills, CA 90211. Quarterly, $7.50/year.

Television/Radio Age. Television Editorial Corporation, 666 Fifth Avenue, New York, NY 10019. Biweekly, $15.00/year.

Variety. Variety, Inc., 154 West 46 Street, New York, NY 10036. Weekly, $30.00/year.

Videography. United Business Publications, Inc., 750 Third Avenue, New York, NY 10017. Monthly, $10.00/year.

RESOURCES FOR TEACHERS

Allen, Don. *The Electric Humanities*. Dayton, OH: Pflaum/Standard, 1971. 276 pp. $5.95 paper.

Anderson, Chuck. *The Electric Journalist: An Introduction to Video.* New York: Praeger Publishers, 1974. 136 pp. $6.50 cloth.

Brown, Les, and Marks, Selma. *Electric Media.* New York: Harcourt Brace Jovanovich, Inc., 1974. 160 pp.

Brown, Roland G. *A Bookless Curriculum.* Dayton, OH: Pflaum/Standard, 1972. 134 pp. $3.96 paper.

Byars, Betsy. *The TV Kid,* illus. Richard Cuffari. New York: Viking Press, 1976. 123 pp. $6.50 cloth.

Center for Understanding Media, Inc. *Doing the Media: A Portfolio of Activities and Resources.* New York: Center for Understanding Media, Inc., 1972. 219 pp. $5.00 paper.

Daigon, Arthur. *Violence U.S.A.* New York: Bantam Books, 1975. 256 pp. $1.95 paper.

Giblin, Thomas R., ed. *Popular Media and the Teaching of English.* Pacific Palisades, CA: Goodyear Publishing Company, Inc., 1972. 276 pp. $7.50 paper.

Goodwin, Mary T., and Pollen, Gerry. *Creative Food Experiences for Children.* Washington, D.C.: Center for Science in the Public Interest, 1974. 191 pp. $4.00 paper.

Heintz, Ann Christine. *Persuasion.* Chicago: Loyola University Press, 1974. 224 pp. $3.20 paper; teacher's guide available.

Heintz, Ann Christine; Reuter, Laurence M.; and Conley, Elizabeth. *Mass Media: A Worktext in the Processes of Modern Communication.* Chicago: Loyola University Press, 1975. 240 pp. $3.50 paper; teacher's guide available.

Katz, Deborah, and Goodwin, Mary T. *Food: Where Nutrition, Politics and Culture Meet.* Washington, D.C.: Center for Science in the Public Interest, 1976. 214 pp. $4.50 paper.

Kuhns, William. *Exploring Television.* Chicago: Loyola University Press, 1975. 240 pp. $3.50 paper; teacher's guide available.

Littell, Joseph F., ed. *Coping with Television.* Evanston, IL: McDougal Littell & Company, 1973. 213 pp. $3.87 paper.

Littell, Joseph F., ed. *Coping with the Mass Media.* Evanston, IL: McDougal Littell & Company, 1972. 156 pp. $3.87 paper.

Mitchell, Wanda. *Televising Your Message: An Introduction to Television as Communication.* Skokie, IL: National Textbook Company, 1974. 206 pp. $4.95 paper.

Moyes, Norman B.; White, David Manning; et al. *Journalism in the Mass Media.* Lexington, MA: Ginn and Company, 1970. 522 pp. $7.92 cloth; laboratory manual and teacher's guide available.

Pember, Don R. *Mass Media in America.* Chicago: Science Research Associates, Inc., 1974. 380 pp. $7.95 paper.

Postman, Neil. *Television and the Teaching of English.* New York: Appleton-Century-Crofts, Inc., 1961. 138 pp.

Potter, Rosemary Lee. *New Season: The Positive Use of Commercial Television with Children.* Columbus, OH: Charles E. Merrill, 1976. 126 pp. $3.95 paper.

Rice, Susan, and Mukerji, Rose, eds. *Children are Centers for Understanding Media.* Washington, D.C.: Association for Childhood Education International, 1973. 89 pp. $3.95 paper.

Schramm, Wilbur. *Big Media, Little Media.* Beverly Hills, CA: Sage Publications, 1977. 313 pp.

Schrank, Jeffrey. *TV Action Book.* Evanston, IL: McDougal Littell & Company, 1974. 127 pp. $2.25 paper.

Seeing Through Commercials. A fifteen-minute, 16mm color film with sound which illustrates and discusses advertising techniques for the primary grades. Los Angeles: Vision Films, 1976. Rental, $25.00; purchase, $225.00.

Six Billion $$$ Sell: A Child's Guide to TV Commercials. A fifteen-minute, 16mm color film with sound on TV advertising for grades 4-8. Mt. Vernon, NY: Consumer Reports Films, 1976. Rental, $25.00; purchase, $220.00.

Sohn, David A., ed. *Good Looking: Film Studies, Short Films and Filmmaking.* Philadelphia: North American Publishing Company, 1976. 238 pp. $5.95 paper.

Sugergoop. A thirteen-minute color sound film on television advertising for the elementary grades. Los Angeles: Churchill Films, 1975. Rental, $18.00; purchase, $190.00.

TV: The Anonymous Teacher. A fifteen-minute color sound film on children and television. New York: United Methodist Communication, 1976. Distributed by Mass Media Ministries, Baltimore, MD. Rental, $20.00; purchase, $225.00.

Teaching Tools for Consumer Education. A monthly service from Consumers Union. Mount Vernon, NY: Consumers Union. Available without charge with a class subscription to *Consumer Reports.*

Television and Values. Palatine, IL: Learning Seed Company, 1976. A multimedia kit including filmstrip and cassette, project cards, texts, and teaching guide. $38.60.

Television, Police and the Law. A curriculum including teacher's guide and spirit masters. Chicago: Prime Time School Television, 1976.

Valdes, Joan, and Crow, Jeanne. *The Media Reader.* Dayton, OH: Pflaum/Standard, 1975. 390 pp. $4.95 paper.

——. *The Media Works and Working with the Media Works.* Dayton OH: Pflaum/Standard, 1973. Text, 282 pp.; logbook, 119 pp. Text, $4.95 paper; logbook, $1.70 paper.

Voelker, Francis H., and Voelker, Ludmila A. *Mass Media: Forces in Our Society.* 2nd ed. New York: Harcourt Brace Jovanovich, Inc., 1975. 431 pp. $6.95 paper.

Wells, Alan. *Mass Media and Society.* Palo Alto, CA: National Press Books, 1972. 407 pp. $6.95 paper.

PERIODICALS FOR TEACHERS

Agency for Instructional Television Newsletter. Agency for Instructional Television, Box A, Bloomington, IN 47401. Free.

American Educator. American Federation of Teachers, AFL-CIO, 11 Dupont Circle N.W., Washington, D.C. 20036. Quarterly, $5.00/year.

Learning. Learning, 530 University Avenue, Palo Alto, CA 94301. Monthly, $10.00/year.

Media and Methods. North American Publishing Company, 134 North 13th Street, Philadelphia, PA 19107. Monthly, $9.00/year.

Prime Time School Television. Suite 810, 120 South LaSalle Street, Chicago, IL 60603. PTST publishes monthly bulletins supplying information for teachers about prime time television programs and their uses as educational resources.

Principal. National Association of Elementary School Principals, 1801 North Moore Street, Arlington, VA 22209.

Teacher. Macmillan Professional Magazines. One Fawcett Place, Greenwich, CT 06830. Monthly, $12.00/year.

Teachers Guides to Television. 699 Madison Avenue, New York, NY 10021. Semi-annual, $3.50/year.

CABLE TELEVISION: GENERAL

Adler, Richard. *The Humanistic Claim on the Cable.* Palo Alto, CA; Aspen Program on Communications and Society, 1973. 60 pp. $2.00 paper.

Adler, Richard, and Baer, Walter S. *The Electronic Box Office: Humanities and Arts on the Cable.* New York: Praeger Publishers, 1974. 139 pp. $12.50 cloth; paper edition available from Aspen Institute, Palo Alto, CA, $3.95.

Baer, Walter S. *Cable Television: A Handbook for Decisionmaking.* Santa Monica, CA: Rand Corporation (R-1133-NSF), 1973. 229 pp. $3.00 paper.

Branscomb, Anne W. "The Cable Fable: Will It Come True?" *Journal of Communication* 25:1 (Winter 1975), pp. 44–56.

The Cabinet Committee on Cable Communications. *CABLE: Report to the President.* Washington, D.C.: U.S. Government Printing Office, 1974. 122 pp. $1.50 paper.

Cable Television: Promise Versus Regulatory Performance. Prepared by the Staff for the Use of the Subcommittee on Communications of the Committee on Interstate and Foreign Commerce, U.S. House of Representatives. Washington, D.C.: U.S. Government Printing Office, 1976. 110 pp. $5.00 paper.

Committee for Economic Development. *Broadcasting and Cable Television —Policies for Diversity and Change.* New York: Committee for Economic Development, 1975. 127 pp. $2.50.

Hallowell, Mary Louise, ed. *Cable Handbook, 1975–1976.* Washington, D.C.: Communications Press, 1975. 303 pp. $6.95 paper.

LeDuc, Don R. *Cable Television and the FCC.* Philadelphia: Temple University Press, 1973. 289 pp. $10.00 cloth.

Park, Rolla Edward, ed. *The Role of Analysis in Regulatory Decision-*

making: The Case of Cable Television. Lexington, MA: Lexington Books, 1973. 114 pp. $9.50 cloth.

Price, Monroe, and Wicklein, John. *Cable Television: A Guide for Citizen Action.* Philadelphia: Pilgrim Press, 1972. 160 pp. $2.95 paper.

A Short Course in Cable. New York: United Church of Christ, 1972. 11 pp. $1.95 paper.

Sloan Commission on Cable Communications. *On the Cable: The Television of Abundance.* New York: McGraw Hill, 1971. 256 pp. $2.95 paper.

Smith, Ralph Lee. *The Wired Nation: Cable TV; the Electronic Communications Highway.* New York: Harper & Row, 1972. 128 pp. $7.00 cloth, $1.95 paper.

Tate, Charles, ed. *Cable Television in the Cities: Community Control, Public Access and Minority Ownership.* Washington, D.C.: The Urban Institute, 1971. 184 pp. $3.95 paper.

Veith, Richard. *Talk-Back TV: Two-Way Cable Television.* Blue Ridge Summit, PA: Tab Books, 1976. 238 pp. $5.95 paper.

CABLE AND EDUCATION

Adler, Richard, and Baer, Walter S. *Aspen Notebook: Cable and Continuing Education.* New York: Praeger Publishers, 1973. 193 pp. $11.00 cloth; paper edition available from Aspen Institute, Palo Alto, CA, $3.95.

Carpenter, Polly. *Cable Television: A Guide for Education Planners.* Santa Monica, CA: Rand Corporation (R-1144-NSF), 1973. 88 pp. $3.00 paper.

——. *Cable Television: Uses in Education.* Santa Monica, CA: Rand Corporation (R-1143-NSF), 1973. 53 pp. $3.00 paper.

Educational Uses of Cable Television. Washington, D.C.: Cable Television Information Center, 1974. Available from Cable Television Information Center, The Urban Institute, Washington, D.C., $2.50 paper.

The Here, Now and Tomorrow of Cable Television in Education. A Study for the Massachusetts Advisory Council on Education, September 1973. ERIC Document ED 086-172. 66 pp.

The National Cable Television Association. *Cable Television and Educa-*

tion: A Report from the Field. Washington, D.C. The National Cable Television Association, 1973. 50 pp. Available from NCTA, Washington, D.C. First copy free; additional copies $.25 each.

National Educational Association. *Schools and Cable Television.* Washington, D.C.: National Education Association, 1971. 66 pp. $2.25 paper.

Shafer, Jon. *Education and Cable TV: A Guide to Franchising and Utilization.* Stanford, CA: ERIC Clearinghouse on Media and Technology, 1973. 47 pp. $2.50 paper.

Appendix F:
ACTFACTS

ACTFACTS

Action for Children's Television (ACT) is a nonprofit national consumer organization based in Newtonville, Massachusetts, working to improve broadcast practices related to children. Through legal action, education, and research, the group is trying to reduce violence and commercialism and encourage quality and diversity on children's television.

ACT's goals are:

to persuade broadcasters and advertisers to provide quality programming designed for children of different ages and diverse racial and ethnic backgrounds;

to encourage the development and enforcement of appropriate guidelines relating to media and children;

to educate and enlighten parents and others involved with children about the importance of television's effects on the child;

to stimulate research, experimentation, and evaluation in the field of children's television;

to develop a network of individuals and institutions to guarantee a broad-based advocacy.

ACT's method of accomplishing its objectives includes:

Educational activities: monitoring, publications, conferences, resource. books, maintenance of a reference library and speakers' bureau, and distribution of materials focusing on the need to reach parents, physicians, teachers, and industry.

Legal actions: petitions to regulatory agencies.

Constituency development: development of a broad-based membership of individuals and institutions.

217

Commissioning research: monitoring studies and analyses of children's TV programs.

ACT's accomplishments include:

Reduction of Saturday morning children's advertising time by 40 percent;

Elimination of vitamin pill advertising on children's programs;

More diversity in TV offerings for children;

Elimination of "host" commercials on children's programs;

Establishment of highly respected ACT Achievement Awards.

Partial List of Endorsers

American Academy of Pediatrics

American Association of University Women

American Educational Theatre Association

American Friends Service Committee

American Group Psychotherapy Association

American Library Association

American Public Health Association

American Society for Preventive Dentistry

Association for Childhood Education International

B'nai B'rith Women

International Reading Association

National Association for Better Broadcasting

National Association for the Education of Young Children

National Catholic Education Association

National Child Research Center

National Children's Center

National Citizens Committee for Broadcasting

National Conference of Christians and Jews

National Education Association

National Health Council

National Organization for Women

National Recreation and Parks Association

Union of American Hebrew Congregations

Board Of Directors

Edward L. Bernays

Peggy Charren

Nancy Codispoti
Dorothy Forbes
Earle K. Moore, Esq.
Priscilla Moulton
Robert E. O'Brien
Daniel A. Phillips
Chester Pierce, M.D.
Frances G. Pratt
Margaret Thomas

Advisory Board

Charles Benton, president, Films, Inc.
John Condry, professor, Cornell University
Joan Ganz Cooney, president, Children's Television Workshop
Dr. John Culkin, director, Center for Understanding Media
Richard Galdston, M.D., psychiatrist, Boston, Mass.
Hyman H. Goldin, associate professor of communications, Boston University School of Public Communications
LaDonna Harris, president, Americans for Indian Opportunity
Mary Gardiner Jones, vice-president, Consumer Affairs, Western Union Telegraph Company
Kenneth Keniston, chairman and director, Carnegie Council on Children
Theodore Ledbetter, president, Urban Communications Group; publisher, "Black Communicator"
Elma Lewis, founder and director, National Center of Afro-American Artists
Richard Lewis, director, Touchstone Center for Children
Marya Mannes, author and commentator
Earle K. Moore, Esq., attorney, Moore, Berson & Lifflander
Grace Olivarez, director, Community Services Administration
Chester Pierce, M.D., professor, education and psychiatry, Harvard University
Letty Cottin Pogrebin, author, editor, *Ms.* magazine
Margret E. Rey, author
Fred Rogers, creator, "Mister Rogers' Neighborhood"
Albert J. Solnit, M.D., Sterling Professor of Pediatrics and Psychiatry; director of Yale University Child Study Center

ACT CHRONOLOGY

January 1968	Informal meetings, discussions, and research concerning children's television. Aims clarified.
Spring 1969	Monitoring of Romper Room for four weeks. Petition circulated protesting host selling and using child participants to demonstrate products. Met with station and program producers at WHDH-TV, Boston.
February 5, 1970	Met with six of seven members of the Federal Communications Commission to talk about need for overall regulation of children's TV and to present petition to eliminate ads from children's programs.
Spring 1970	ACT filed briefs with FCC on ACT petition. Support sought by ACT from public and national organizations.
March 1970	ACT commissioned study "Programming and Advertising Practices in Television Directed to Children" by Ralph Jennings.
	ACT commissioned pilot study "Mothers' Attitudes Toward Children's Television Programs and Commercials" by Daniel Yankelovitch, Inc. Both studies submitted as part of ACT filing to FCC.
October 15, 16, 1970	First National Symposium on Children and Television co-hosted by ACT, Kennedy Memorial Hospital, and Boston University School of Public Communications, at Kennedy Memorial Hospital for Children.
May 1971	ACT commissioned study "Saturday Morning Children's Programming on Boston TV Stations, May–June 1971" by Professor F. Earle Barcus of Boston University School of Public Communications.
Summer 1971	ACT opened office at 46 Austin Street, Newtonville, Massachusetts 02160.
October 18, 1971	Second Symposium on Children and Television, co-sponsored with American Academy of Pediatrics at Palmer House Hotel, Chicago.
December 1971	ACT filed a petition with the FTC to prohibit selling of toys to children on TV.
March 1972	ACT testified at hearings on the Surgeon-General's Report on Television and Social Behavior conducted by Senator John Pastore.
	ACT filed a petition with the FTC to prohibit selling of edibles to children on TV.

April 1972	ACT filed specific complaints with the FTC against three major drug companies for advertising vitamins directly to children.
July 1972	Three major drug companies agreed to end advertising for vitamin pills on children's commercial TV programs in response to ACT's petition. (FTC had not yet acted).
October 1972	Third National Symposium on Children and Television held in cooperation with Yale Child Study Center and Yale School of Art and Architecture, New Haven. First informal meeting of ACT Contacts from across the country. ACT commissioned pilot study analyzing treatment of black and other minority groups on network children's television by BEST (Black Efforts for Soul in Television).
January 1973	National Association of Broadcasters initiated new code rules stating: 1) no host selling on children's programs, and 2) ads on weekend children's programs cut to twelve minutes per hour.
March 1973	ACT filed specific complaints with the FTC against cereal and candy companies and CBS-TV Network for advertising of sugared edibles directed to children, and filed supplement to edibles petition. ACT filed a brief with the FTC on proposed guides advocating the prohibition of endorsements and testimonials in advertisements aimed at children.
Fall 1973	ACT-commissioned study, "Children's Television: The Economics of Exploitation," by Dr. William H. Melody, published by Yale University Press.
March 1974	ACT and other consumer representatives submitted to the FTC a compromise code of guidelines for children's advertising. Industry called compromise unacceptable.
April 1974	ACT held its fourth annual conference, an international Festival of Children's Television, at the Kennedy Center for the Performing Arts in Washington, D.C.
June 1974	In response to ACT pressure, the Television Code Review Board of the National Association of Broad-

casters recommended that by December 31 the amount of commercial time be cut from twelve to ten minutes per hour, and to nine and a half minutes per hour on weekends by 1975.

September 1974   ACT submitted comments to the FTC on Proposed Guidelines Concerning Use of Premiums on Television Advertisements Directed to Children.

November 1974   FCC issued report and policy statement on children's television programs, but failed to issue any rules.

February 1975   ACT filed law suit charging FTC inaction on food advertising petition, in U.S. District Court, Washington, D.C.

June 1975   In response to an ACT request, WDCA-TV, an independent station in Washington, D.C., withdrew a two-week series of fifty-four fireworks commercials scheduled to air on afternoon and early evening children's programs prior to July 4th.

October 1975   ACT filed a petition for rulemaking with the FTC to prohibit the advertising of vitamins on children's and family television programs. As part of the filing ACT registered a formal complaint and request for injunctive relief against Hudson Pharmaceutical Corporation, manufacturer of Spider-Man Vitamins.

November 1975   ACT held its Fifth National Symposium on Children and Television, "Children's Television and the Arts," at the Memorial Arts Center in Atlanta.

November 1975   ACT filed a brief for an appeal of the FCC Policy Statement on Children's TV in the U.S. Court of Appeals in Washington, D.C.

December 1975   ACT released "Weekend Commercial Children's Television" and "Television in the Afterschool Hours," studies by Dr. F. Earle Barcus dealing with children's programming on network and independent stations.

February 1976   In response to ACT's complaints about a series of fireworks ads which were scheduled on WDCA-TV, the NAB Code Review Board voted to ban all televised fireworks advertising effective February 1, 1976.

March 1976   ACT and the NCCB filed an *amicus curiae* brief critical of the Family Hour, supporting the Writers Guild of America, west in its suit against the FCC and the networks on this issue.

May 1976   ACT filed a formal complaint with the FTC against Mars, Inc., for its prominently advertised Milky Way commercial, which advocates a child's consumption of the candy bar "wherever you are. . . . at work, rest, or play."

ACT participated in a joint FCC-FTC panel on the advertising of over-the-counter drugs on television.

September 1976 ACT released "Pre-Christmas Advertising to Children," a study by Dr. F. Earle Barcus comparing advertising on children's TV programs broadcast in April and November of 1975.

Responding to ACT's formal complaint against Hudson Pharmaceutical Corporation, the FTC issued a consent order prohibiting the company from "directing its advertising for Spider-Man and other children's vitamins to child audiences."

Oral argument in ACT's suit against the FCC was presented before the U.S. Court of Appeals in Washington by attorneys Earle K. Moore and Henry Geller.

September 1976 ACT was cited in Ann Landers' syndicated newspaper column and received over 25,000 inquiries seeking information concerning violence on children's television.

October 1976   ACT received the American Academy of Pediatrics Distinguished Public Service Award.

November 1976   U.S. District Judge Warren J. Ferguson of Los Angeles Federal Court supported ACT's contention by ruling that the Family Viewing Hour violates the First Amendment.

ACT held its Sixth National Symposium on Children and Television, "Products and Programs: The Child as Consumer," in Cambridge in cooperation with the Harvard Graduate School of Education.

December 1976   ACT filed a complaint with the FTC against Hasbro Industries, Inc., for using deceptive practices to advertise its Bulletman toy in television commercials directed to children.

April 1977   ACT filed a petition with the FTC to prohibit the advertising of candy to children on television.

May 1977   ACT announced publication of its resource hand-

	book, *Promise and Performance: ACT's Guide to TV Programming for Children, Volume I: Children with Special Needs.*
June 1977	ACT filed a formal complaint with the FTC against General Foods Corporation for its TV commercials for Cocoa Pebbles.
July 1977	FTC chairman Michael Pertschuk met with ACT and fourteen national groups on proposed regulation of TV candy ads. ACT sought FTC injunction against Ralston Purina for a fast-food sweepstakes campaign featuring child actor Rodney Allen Rippy.
August 1977	ACT filed a formal FTC complaint against Ralston Purina's advertising campaign for Cookie Crisp, a presweetened cereal.
November 1977	ACT held a research workshop, "Televised Role Models and Young Adolescents," at the Harvard Graduate School of Education. FTC chairman Michael Pertschuk was a featured speaker.
January 1978	ACT announced the advisory board for its two-year project designed to encourage innovative arts programming on children's television.
February 1978	ACT filed a petition with the FCC to ultimately eliminate all advertising from children's TV programs.
April 1978	The FTC initiated a rule-making procedure which will consider the elimination of TV advertising directed to children under eight and a ban on ads for highly sugared snacks directed to children under twelve.

For more information about Action for Children's Television, fill out the form below and send this page to ACT, 46 Austin Street, Newtonville, MA 02160. If you wish, complete the questionnaire, so that ACT can find out what really concerns you about children's television.

I would like more information about ACT.

Name: _____

Address: _____

I am particularly concerned about _____

_____

_____

1. I am _____ _____ _____ of _____ children, who are
      (mother), (father), (other) (how many)
   _____ .
   (ages)
2. The following refers to my child(ren) (give ages) _____
   Please answer questions in a different color ink for each child between the ages of two and eleven.
3. On an average weekday, how many hours of TV does your child watch? Saturday? _____ ; Sunday? _____; After 8 P.M.? _____ .
4. Do you think there are enough programs in your area designed specifically for children? Yes _____ ; No _____ .
5. How often do you watch TV with your child?
   Never _____; Occasionally _____ ; Often _____; Almost always _____ .
6. Which programs does your child watch most often?
   _____

   _____

7. In general, how would you rate these programs?
   Excellent _____; Good _____; Fair _____; Poor _____ .
8. How would you rate children's television in general?
   _____

   _____

9. There are commercials on children's TV at present. Would you prefer children's TV to have:
   No commercials? _____ ; Fewer commercials? _____ ; Commercials at the beginning and end of programs only? _____ ; No change in the present system? _____ .

10. How often has your child asked you to buy a cereal advertised on TV?
   Never _____ ; Occasionally _____ ; Frequently _____ .
   Did you buy the cereal?
   Were you satisfied with the purchase? Yes _____ ; No _____ .
   If not, why not? _____

   _____

11. How often has your child requested a toy advertised on TV?

   _____

   Did you buy the toy? Yes _____ ; No _____ .
   Were you satisfied with the item purchased? Yes _____ ; No _____ .
   If not, why not? _____

   _____

12. What other comments do you have about children's TV?   _____

   _____

   _____

   _____

THE AUTHOR

Evelyn Kaye, co-founder and first president of Action for Children's Television (ACT), also served as executive director and publicity director of the organization until 1974. Most recently she has devoted full time to writing. She is the author of three books and writes frequently about media, travel, and the arts for magazines and newspapers.